Sonny Bill Williams

The Story of Rugby's New Superstar

SONNY BILL WILLIAMS

THE STORY OF RUGBY'S NEW SUPERSTAR

John Matheson/Celebrity Portraits

CONTENTS

1,000-MEGAWATT DEBUT 11

BREAKING OUT 39

CHASING THE ALL BLACK DREAM 63

PUSHING THE BOUNDARIES. 99

STATISTICS. 140

1,000-MEGAWATT DEBUT

EVEN before Wayne Smith was rehired as an All Blacks coach he stressed the need for New Zealand's rugby bosses to 'think outside of the square' when it came to rebuilding the national team.

Smith — talking to this reporter — reacted to the devastation that was the All Blacks' semifinal exit at the 2003 World Cup campaign by suggesting rugby league was a breeding ground for possible rugby recruits. At the time Smith, the All Blacks' head coach in 2000 and most of 2001, was in charge of the English club Northampton. He'd spent many hours watching the likes of Kiwis league stars Robbie Paul and Lesley Vainikolo tear it up in the Super League. And he was convinced that duo, and others, could help the All Blacks.

'We can't afford to be insular,' Smith said. 'When it comes to rugby New Zealanders tend to be a bit arrogant. We're convinced that we know it all. We don't always think that we can learn from what's happening on the other side of the world, let alone what's happening in the rival code. We need to change that way of thinking if we're ever to move forward. We have to look at a player like Robbie and recognize that having him in New Zealand playing rugby could only help us. We have to be proactive. Because clearly what we are doing at the moment isn't working.'

It was 2004 and soon after doing the interview Smith was hired as Graham Henry's assistant coach alongside Steve Hansen.

Fast forward to 2009. After the All Blacks' quarterfinal exit at the 2007 World Cup, the New Zealand Rugby Union were finally willing to back Smith's brave new vision for the team. Smith, in France to monitor the progress of the injured All Black first-five Dan Carter — who was ensconced in Perpignan at the time — took the opportunity to meet with rugby league exile Sonny Bill Williams. The former Canterbury Bulldog was playing for Toulon and over a quiet cup of coffee Smith laid out the All Blacks' plans for him. Smith would later describe the meeting as the first 'significant' contact between Williams and the Men in Black.

Within days of the meeting Williams re-signed for Toulon — for a year. 'The motivation behind the one-year deal was the improvement that [Sonny] continues to make,' his manager Khoder Nasser said. 'Anyone who has seen him can see the improvement so it makes sense to maximize his value. One way of doing that is signing a one-year deal. Sonny loves a challenge. By having a one-year deal he's highly motivated to make sure at the end of it he's in the best possible position to take advantage of being on the market again.'

It was a major win for Smith and the All Blacks because it meant that come 2010 Williams would be on the market — and with another year of rugby under his belt, Smith hoped, Williams would be in a position to take up the challenge of trying to be an All Black.

And on 29 March the whole world was in on the plan thanks to this reporter's story in the *Sunday News*. The headline blasted across the front page was straightforward enough — *All Blacks plea to Sonny Bill … 'Play For Us at World Cup!'* What wouldn't be straightforward was the journey Williams would have to take before he fulfilled a boyhood dream and donned the All Blacks jersey.

A LONG three years before, Sonny Bill Williams's name would be up in lights for all the wrong reasons. One of the great names of rugby league forecast the goings-on in 2008 which would rob his game of one of its brightest stars and set in motion a rugby route which will culminate at rugby's 2011 World Cup.

The year was 2005 and Phil Gould — the Super Coach who had won the Winfield Cup with Penrith and made a name for himself as one of State of Origin's winningest mentors — had grown tired of the question which would be put to him almost on a daily basis by punters, club administrators, fellow coaches, players or scribes: 'If you sign one player in the game today, who would it be and how much would you pay him?'

'I replied "Sonny Bill Williams and he is worth $1 million a season",' Gould wrote in his *Sun-Herald* column in Australia. 'Obviously, no one can pay Sonny Bill $1 million a year. But that is what he is worth. I have

no doubts that this great young player would provide value for his club and for rugby league at that figure. But the most money any responsible NRL club could pay him under the salary cap is about $300,000 a year if it wants to retain other quality players and ensure the club has the depth and talent to be successful for years to come. If any club, including the Bulldogs, signs him and puts up $300,000 as his contract amount, it will have to live with the rumours and jibes that it is paying him under the table.'

Gould said Williams was the latest in a long list of top-line players finding how restrictive the NRL salary-cap system was. 'Sonny Bill wants to stay with the Bulldogs but faces the very real prospect he may have to leave to earn his true contract value. Not only are the Bulldogs in danger of losing their star player, but rugby league may lose him to another code if someone doesn't change this farcical situation.'

Gould, a long-time critic of the National Rugby League's salary cap, knew then what the rugby league world would discover in 2008 when Williams walked out on his contract with the Canterbury Bulldogs to sign a telephone-digit contract with the French rugby club Toulon. Money, or a lack of it, would eventually cost the sport the man-child who'd given the game — and in particular the Bulldogs — a reason to smile again after the endless sex scandals and salary-cap abuse which had cast a giant shadow over rugby league.

Williams had reached those lofty heights after a barnstorming beginning to his rugby league career — the high point coming a year before Gould's comments when he played a key role in the Bulldogs' march to glory in the NRL's Grand Final in 2004, the same year he debuted for the Canterbury-Bankstown side's first-grade team.

Wayne Smith, the All Blacks assistant coach, knew recruiting the likes of Sonny Bill Williams would be crucial to any future success of the national team.

Super Coach Phil Gould, the former Penrith and NSW boss, was one of the first to promote Sonny Bill Williams as a $1 million player — and worth every cent.

Williams had joined Canterbury in 2002 as a lock forward. He had an excellent pedigree, as his maternal grandfather, Bill Woolsey, is spoken of in revered tones as the toughest player ever to wear the Kiwi jersey. A former boxer, Woolsey was never backward in his role as an enforcer in the City Newton front row and was a legend of more than one riotous after-match function. He epitomized everything about the league hard men of the 1950s and 1960s. Williams's father's family has a Samoan background and also played rugby of one code or the other to add to the mix, but it was Williams's mum who took him down to Auckland's renowned Mount Albert club as an eight-year-old.

John Ackland — who would go on to be the New Zealand Warriors' premiership-winning under-20 coach — was a talent scout for the club at the time. He spotted him at Owairaka Primary School, and after a few years at the Marist club and at the age of 15 he became Canterbury's youngest signing, moving to Sydney to complete his education. Once he'd finished high school he was signed on a $A5,000 contract, lived in a home with six other budding

players (including Sydney Roosters' modern-day star Nate Myles), made his own sandwiches and had to clean the bird poo off the seats at Belmore Oval to earn his keep.

Brad Clyde — the Canberra Raiders great — was the Bulldogs' marketing manager at the time and remembers Williams's 'big Poison haircut. It was like the big Van Halen piece of work and then he had the comb rub through that to keep it out of his eyes. I thought, "He must want a tough time playing footy because everyone is just going to pull on that hair of his." It took two games for me to realize he had something special.'

Williams quickly established himself as a regular member of the Bulldogs' Jersey Flegg team which competed in Sydney's under-20 competition — he was named the age-group player of the year — and played in the Preliminary Final against St George Illawarra in his first year. The following season he was promoted to the club's Premier League set-up and played for New South Wales' under-19s team before a shoulder injury ended his chances of a first-grade call-up.

He was a compulsive offloader in his early days but trained hard to lose the habit. He also liked a drink with the boys after training. But after an impressive pre-season in 2004 when he won his way into the NRL side he made a decision not to touch a drop of the hard stuff until the Bulldogs' season was over — something that didn't happen until they knocked off the Roosters in the 2004 Grand Final.

Said Clyde: 'He was very focused about what he wanted to achieve and he wasn't easily distracted. … He wanted to be as good a player as possible.'

Even before his first game for the first-grade side, Laurie Daley — another of Canberra's greats — predicted Williams 'will be the best player New Zealand has ever produced. He is awesome. Big, strong, quick on his feet and skilful. He will be one of the greats.' Daley made the call after seeing SBW torment St George Illawarra on the Gold Coast in a trial game two weeks before the NRL season.

His try-scoring debut at centre as an 18-year-old against Parramatta at the start of the 2004 season was something of a dream start to his NRL career. He was completely unstoppable in the first half, which set the platform for the 48–14 win. Williams had been mainly used as a back-rower in the lower grades the previous year, but with Ben Harris injured and Matt Utai suspended, Williams was given his chance in the centres. The club website's editor compared his debut to that of club great Steve Mortimer. 'Back in 1976, the front cover on *Rugby League Week* said "A Star Is Born" when Mortimer emerged on the scene,' the report said. 'The ... hype Mortimer received 28 years ago will be the same for Williams as he breathed life into the Bulldogs. Canterbury have produced one of the finest opening 40 minutes of football [and] the match witnessed the emergence of a future superstar in Sonny Bill Williams.'

David Leggat — the *New Zealand Herald*'s respected sports scribe — couldn't contain himself either after being exposed to the prodigy for the first time. 'There's something special about being able to say "I was there" when a fresh sporting star blinks on the horizon,' he wrote in his editorial. 'Think Michael Jones' test debut against Italy at the start of the victorious 1987 Rugby World Cup; think 17-year-old Boris Becker becoming the youngest Wimbledon champion in 1985; think English hero Ian Botham bagging five wickets on his test cricket debut against Australia in 1977; and — as this is leading to the 13-a-side code — old-time leaguies are still prone to get misty-eyed when they remember an 18-year-old Dennis Williams cutting the British defence to pieces on debut in 1971. So it might just be with Sonny Bill Williams, an 18-year-old tank not long out of Mt Albert Grammar, who exploded on the NRL stage with a 1000-megawatt debut for the Bulldogs against the Parramatta Eels. Williams set up one try with a surging 60 m run, had a hand in another try and scored one of his own; Laurie Daley might just be on the money.'

Sonny Bill Williams in action for the Canterbury Bulldogs in 2004 — he would go on to win the NRL title with them that year.

Williams would become a key figure in the Bulldogs' pack by the time they reached, and won, the Grand Final. Indeed, while he started the final from the bench, he provided one of the game's great highlights — a bone-crunching highlight-reel hit on Chris Flannery. His performances have been so impressive that the likes of Canterbury greats Paul Dunn and David Gillespie were rating Williams one of the Bulldogs' all-time great forwards. Dunn even went as far as to brand him 'a once in a generation player', placing him in the same calibre as Daley and Brad Fittler.

And the great Kiwis coach of the 1980s and Manly and Queensland coach in the 1990s Graham Lowe — never one to hand out compliments unless they're warranted — offered perhaps the most generous praise of all. 'During my coaching career, I was fortunate to have guided three of the best players of all time — Mark Graham, Ellery Hanley and Wally Lewis,' he said. 'I do not say it lightly, but I think Williams will turn out to be better than each of them.'

In the middle of it all in 2004, SBW had had a test debut against Australia — when Daniel Anderson selected him for the Kiwis as he became New Zealand's youngest-ever player and was reportedly spotted collecting teammates' autographs in the dressing room. But the autograph-hunting at North Harbour Stadium didn't begin until he'd played a significant role in only the Kiwis' second-ever draw (16–16) with the Kangaroos. While brothers Louis

DOGS IN HEAVEN

Steve Folkes' Canterbury Bulldogs won rugby league's toughest comp for the eighth time in 2004 when they defeated the Sydney Roosters 16–13 at Telstra Stadium. Sonny Bill Williams was in the Bulldogs' line-up, starting the Grand Final on the interchange bench.

Sydney Roosters	Position	Canterbury Bulldogs
Anthony Minichiello	FB	Luke Patten
Shannon Hegarty	WG	Hazem El Masri
Ryan Cross	C	Ben Harris
Justin Hodges	C	Willie Tonga
Chris Walker	WG	Matt Utai
Brad Fittler (capt.)	5/8	Braith Anasta
Brett Finch	HB	Brent Sherwin
Jason Cayless	PR	Mark O'Meley
Craig Wing	HK	Adam Perry
Adrian Morley	PR	Roy Asotasi
Michael Crocker	SR	Willie Mason
Craig Fitzgibbon	SR	Andrew Ryan (capt.)
Chris Flannery	L	Tony Grimaldi
Peter Cusack	Bench	Corey Hughes
Anthony Tupou	Bench	Sonny Bill Williams
Chad Robinson	Bench	Reni Maitua
Ned Catic	Bench	Jonathan Thurston
Ricky Stuart	Coach	Steve Folkes

SCORE

13		16
Tries to Walker and Minichiello		Tries to Utai (2) and El Masri
Goals (2) Fitzgibbon		Goals (2) El Masri
Field Goal (1) Finch		
Halftime: 6–13	Referee: Bill Harrigan	

Happy Frank: Kiwis coach Frank Endacott tipped Sonny Bill Williams as a 'once in a generation' player in his Kiwis debut year in 2004.

and Vinnie Anderson and wing Francis Meli were try-scorers in the thriller, it was Williams who had set the tone for the combative contest with two bone-shattering hits and elusive running which threatened to break the Kangaroos' line with his every touch of the ball.

By the time he'd got to Huddersfield to play Great Britain three weeks later he'd been outstanding in two more tests. First was against the Kangaroos, winning the man-of-the-match award in the 16-all draw in Auckland. Next he offered a British audience the first glimpse of his class with a stunningly subtle pass to lay on the first try of the Tri-Nations test against the Kangaroos at Loftus Road in London.

Before the Huddersfield test, former Kiwis coach Frank Endacott was asked to offer an opinion on

Sonny Bill Williams (left) cut an impressive figure in his first year in the Kiwis. So much so that Kiwi legend Dean Bell (above) put him in the same stratosphere as All Black great Jonah Lomu when it came to ability and hype. FOLLOWING PAGES: Sonny Bill Williams in action against Great Britain in 2004.

the 19-year-old wunderkind for the *Guardian*'s UK audience. 'Put it this way, if he was a racehorse, you'd already be lining him up for the Arc de Triomphe,' said Endacott, who had helped unearth and then mould the great Stacey Jones. 'It can be dangerous to say this about someone so young, but I can tell you he's going to be something very special. Players like him come along once every 10 or 15 years, if that.'

Another with a connection to the Kiwis, former Wigan, Auckland Warriors and New Zealand skipper

Dean Bell, was just as emphatic in his praise. 'I've been speaking to people back in New Zealand,' he said, 'and they tell me that where in the past it's been all Jonah Lomu and the All Blacks, at the moment the name on everybody's lips is Sonny Bill. The young kids want to get their hair cut like Sonny Bill, such is the interest surrounding him. And it's not the sort of name you forget, is it? He's one of the most exciting talents I've ever seen and, just as important, he seems to have the temperament to handle it. I guess being

'It can be dangerous to say this about someone so young, but I can tell you he's going to be something very special. Players like him come along once every 10 or 15 years, if that.'

Steve Folkes (above) would become a major player in the goings-on of Sonny Bill Williams in his last days under his stewardship at Canterbury-Bankstown. Tension between the player and his coach would ultimately be one of the reasons given for SBW's departure to France.

with Canterbury has helped him in that way. They've always been a mentally tough sort of club.'

And Robbie Paul — then Williams's Kiwis teammate — couldn't help but wax lyrical about SBW on his arrival in the UK where Paul was plying his trade in the Super League. 'The guy is a freak of nature,' Paul said. 'He's an exceptional athlete. He can step brilliantly off either foot and he's lightning quick. At 6 ft 4 in and 16 stone, his speed and agility are outstanding.'

St Helens — the famed British club — were so impressed with Williams that they tried to woo him to the United Kingdom in 2005. The deal included a house, car and annual return flights to Australia. St Helens also signed off on an agreement which would allow Williams to secure a personal sponsorship deal worth up to £100,000 a season — all of which would be serious breaches of the NRL's salary cap if repeated in Australia.

But Williams and his then representative, brothers Chris and Gavin Orr, knew the value of building his 'brand' in the toughest league competition in the world. The NRL — while hamstrung by a salary cap — was still *the* place to be for anyone aspiring to be the world's best. And that undoubtedly was a goal for Williams.

After winning the Newcomer of the Year at the International Rugby League Awards dinner in England, the 19-year-old's Bulldogs contract was upgraded to a reported $A400,000 a year at the beginning of 2005. His managers were talking about him in the same breath as rugby superstar Jonah Lomu. Williams was starring in a TV advert with Australian cricketer Brett Lee and triathlete Loretta Harrop promoting an energy drink, and a deal with Nike was in the works and a deal with Pepsi signed. The agreement with the soft-drink giant was part of a A$3 million advertising campaign which saw his image plastered on more than 50 billboards and 5000 bus stops across Australia. Previous 'Pepsi Ambassadors' had included footballer Harry Kewell, tennis player Mark Philippoussis and 2004 Miss Universe Jennifer Hawkins. 'We'd like to see him get to where Jonah Lomu was,' Gavin Orr said. 'In time, I think he can be on the same level, in terms of profile, as [swimming legend] Ian Thorpe.'

Williams, though, wasn't able to contribute to his growing legend in his sophomore season as it was ruined by injury — he managed only five games in the NRL as he began an 18-month battle with knee and ankle injuries. But his profile remained high, courtesy of a charge for drink driving. The Bulldogs imposed an A$5000 instant fine after he was charged with a low-range drink-driving offence. 'I would never hop behind

Sonny Bill Williams's first association with European football came in 2005 when he helped promote the Bulldogs' World Club Challenge game against the Leeds Rhinos. He is pictured with Leeds's Kevin Sinfield (left) and Danny McGuire.

the wheel if I thought I was drunk, obviously I had one too many and I'm not using that as an excuse,' Williams told a press conference. 'What I did was irresponsible. I have let a lot of people down and I've let myself and my family down. This week I did find out I would miss the rest of the year and I would not be going on the Tri-Nations [tour]. But I'm not using that as an excuse. It is a bit tough when you're training for five months and you find out your season is finished. But there's no way I'll be using that as an excuse. I am totally disappointed in myself for my actions. This is definitely one of the lowest points in my life, especially after trying to get a good image out there and having a strong fan base, especially with the young kids. I am going to cop the fine from the club and what the court hands out to me.' The court would eventually suspend his licence for five months and fine him $A700.

All that was forgotten, however, when he returned to the field and was back to his best and earning every cent of his pay packet in 2006 with eight tries in his 21 games. He returned to the Canterbury backline to fill in for injured centres Andrew Emelio and Willie Tonga and ended the season playing in the Preliminary Final against Brisbane as a lock.

The hype around the phenomenon that was Sonny Bill Williams was back at fever pitch as the 21-year-old competed for back-page headlines with game greats like Andrew Johns and Darren Lockyer. In August 2006 he sat down with the *Herald Sun*'s James Hooper and opened up about his struggle to adapt to life in the fishbowl of professional rugby league and his desire to break into the Bulldogs' starting side as opposed to continuing to start from the bench.

'I usually say I'm happy being in the side but obviously every player wants to start,' Williams said. 'I wouldn't mind starting, too, but the team is going

'I usually say I'm happy being in the side but obviously every player wants to start.'

so well at the moment. I'm not embarrassed to be on the bench with the forward pack we've got, but I would like to start. But who are you going to drop? I'm happy because the team is going good.'

Williams — cast in the role of the shy Polynesian superstar-in-the-making (think: Lomu, Michael Jones and Manu Vatuvei) — would, of course, have preferred to be a man with no profile. But any hopes of that had to be cast aside, not just because of his undoubted talent but also because he was headlining a new breed of exciting rugby league players — the charge of the Polynesian brigade. Others who would occupy the top rank in that race would include the likes of Israel Folau, Fuifui Moimoi and Jarryd Hayne.

Before them all there were men like Brownie Paki who, in 1923, became the first Polynesian player to play rugby league in Australia when he signed for St George. Walter Mussing, a wing with St George in the 1940s, followed, and he in turn paved the way for the famed Fijian brothers Apisai and Inosi Toga, who played for the same club in the late 1960s and 1970s. Oscar Danielson, a forward with Newtown in the 1970s, is widely considered to be the first Samoan-

born player to play professionally, and he set the stage for the likes of Cronulla's Kurt and Dane Sorensen, Olsen Filipaina (Balmain, Eastern Suburbs and North Sydney) and Norths' Fred Ah Kuoi.

More recently players like Nigel Vagana, Ali Lauitiiti and Monty Betham played the role of the humble Island star — all of them more comfortable among family and friends than under the spotlight. That's the mould Williams was cast in — still embarrassed when people asked for his autograph or pointed when they recognized him in public.

'It's overwhelming and I still get shy now when people come up and ask for signatures,' he said. 'It's all right when I'm by myself, but when I'm around the boys or family, I get a bit embarrassed. But I guess it comes with the territory of being a first-grade footy player and being in the spotlight. In a perfect world I would just play footy, have no profile and just fly under the radar.'

One of the unforeseen advantages of his time away from the game with injuries was that it coincided with the emergence of a new brigade of stars including Benji Marshall and Greg Inglis. He was happy for them

Steve Folkes takes a training session with the Bulldogs. Sonny Bill Williams would never see out his contract at the club as a career in rugby beckoned.

to have the spotlight he'd had in 2004. But his form was such that at the end of the 2006 season he was back at the top of the rugby league's 'most wanted' list.

Although he was contracted to the Bulldogs for 2007, the Orr brothers were seeking a contract extension for him to remain at Belmore, preferably for a further three years. 'There's been a lot of interest in him, but we haven't been prepared to sit down with anybody yet,' Gavin Orr said. 'He likes the Bulldogs and they have never done anything wrong by him. If he's going to stay with the Dogs, he'd be looking for a longer deal than just two years.'

Part of Williams's negotiations with Canterbury revolved around which position he would play. In 2006, Bulldogs coach Steve Folkes shifted him between the interchange bench, the centres and the back row, with the last his preferred position. 'We've been short in the backs so he chucked me out there for a while,

but I'd like to stay in the forwards,' Williams said at the time. 'You always want to be out there when it's on early. You want to be there when all the big hits are going on.'

Something else that was going on at the time was, for the first time, the New Zealand Rugby Union taking an interest in signing Williams. Rugby signing league players had become something of the norm at the time — the Welsh had Iestyn Harris, England went for Jason Robinson and the Wallabies had bought Lote Tuqiri, Mat Rogers and Wendell Sailor, the last four all playing in the 2003 World Cup final.

Graham Lowe, writing in the *New Zealand Herald*, was adamant the All Blacks needed to take the plunge. 'Sonny Bill has the ability, like Mark Graham had, to comfortably make the change to rugby and become the next (with due respect to Richie McCaw) Michael Jones. He's probably lacking the bulk we have become accustomed to in the All Black jersey but,

As far back as 2007, NZRU CEO Steve Tew (then the deputy CEO) was making enquires about the status of Sonny Bill Williams as he dreamt of bringing the phenomenon into the All Blacks' fold.

when it comes to talent, he'd fit like a glove. I'd find it difficult to accept that he shouldn't be on their radar, even if he is tied up with the Dogs at present. The All Blacks are winning but are in danger of being very easily read, by Australia in particular, when it comes to the World Cup [in 2007]. The Bulldogs could never hope to compete in a bidding war, if it ever came to that, with the rugby union for a player like Sonny Bill. Because, although they are one of the wealthiest clubs in Australia, their hands are tied by the salary cap. If I was Graham Henry, I'd be saying to [NZRU CEO] Chris Moller: "That's the player I need to make

sure we win this World Cup — get him for me."'

Moller's deputy at the time, Steve Tew, admitted the NZRU had made enquires about SBW. 'Sonny Bill Williams is obviously a talent and we thought it would be appropriate just to check and see if there was any interest or not,' Tew said. 'The initial approach came from someone in the Sonny Bill camp to one of our coaches. I think they were just generally checking options and he was at the stage of his career where he wants to think things through.'

It would be Folkes, though, who got his man when Williams signed a five-year deal believed to be worth over A$2 million in March 2007. Williams was initially offered a three-year deal for A$1.5 million but asked Bulldogs officials to extend the contract so he could remain a Canterbury player until the end of 2012.

Williams said the decision to remain at the club and turn down offers from the UK came after a heart-to-heart with his father. 'I pretty much came to this decision last night talking to my old man. Growing up, we didn't have much and with the signing after five years I'm pretty sure I will have some for me and some for my family. It was a big decision and I always wanted a five-year deal. I have not been sleeping too well the last couple of weeks. I don't want to go through this ever again. I want to get myself and my family a good future.'

IF the rugby league fraternity had thought they'd seen the best of Sonny Bill Williams — and many had written him off because of his habit of picking up injuries — his stellar season in 2007 would propel him into the stratosphere normally reserved for rugby league gods.

Before he could attempt to take his place at league's top table, though, Williams had to deal with a number of off-field distractions. First up it was the embarrassment of being caught on camera in a compromising position with Australian ironwoman Candice Falzon in a hotel toilet cubicle. The incident dominated front pages in Sydney as Williams and his New Zealand girlfriend Genna Shaw went public to vow their year-long relationship would survive the scandal. Shaw, a former Auckland bar manager who moved to Sydney in 2006 to live with Williams, said it had been 'a very tough week' but she would forgive him. 'I am hurt. But this can only make us stronger. It would have to make us stronger as a couple, wouldn't it?' she told the *Sun-Herald* newspaper. 'I believe him when he says he doesn't know what he was doing or where he was going. I would leave him if I didn't believe that.'

Shaw and Williams went to the same primary school in Auckland but only became a couple when they met again after a New Zealand Warriors game against Williams's Bulldogs. Williams told the paper he had no memory of the Falzon incident. 'She's the most important thing in my life. Football's here for a lot of my life, but I want Genna involved for all of it,' Williams said. 'I know it sounds so stupid saying I can't remember. But I can honestly say, I don't remember anything. I'm ashamed and embarrassed. I've really let down all my loved ones, especially Genna. I'm glad she has stuck by me.'

There was also a fine for urinating in public. And in the best traditions of Jonah Lomu, he was also guilty of lashing out at a photographer who trained his camera on him for longer than Williams felt comfortable. The difference between the two incidents, though, was telling. When Lomu broke the *New Zealand Herald*'s Kenny Rodger's camera it was after a Blues practice. When SBW hit out and broke a Sydney photographer's $15,000 camera he was exiting King's Cross's Hugo's nightclub. Williams was also fined after he was caught speeding. BMW, one of his personal sponsors, reacted by ending their association with him.

'There are people out there who are just waiting for the players to stuff up,' Williams said of the off-field attention that he and other NRL stars received. 'I've had my own indiscretions, but I think the players just need to know that there are people out there who want them to stuff up.' Still, he wasn't making excuses as he vowed to take 'drastic measures' to end the incidents. 'I know the bad publicity I've had has all been alcohol-related. I'll be seeking professional help with regards to alcohol and, until the club and I feel this is under control, I'll be off the drink.'

With all that off-field turmoil, in retrospect it makes his 14 tries from 21 outings with the Bulldogs that year look all the more remarkable. Indeed, it was only two weeks after his pledge to get off the drink that he put in one of the most remarkable performances in the history of the NRL.

The occasion was the Round 16 game against

One of Sonny Bill Williams's best games as a Bulldog came against the Sydney Roosters: Williams scored two tries and set up two more in a performance Steve Folkes described as 'his best ever'.

the Sydney Roosters at Telstra Stadium — a game the Bulldogs would win 38–6 and a night when Canterbury's coach Steve Folkes said he couldn't remember seeing Williams play a better game of rugby league and doubted he ever would again.

'Stepping up in the absence of NSW stars Willie Mason, Andrew Ryan and Hazem El Masri — and with Mark O'Meley suspended — Williams tore apart the Roosters, scoring two tries, going within centimetres of two more and setting up another with a trademark flick over the top of the defender that he labelled a "fluke",' a press report said. 'The night belonged to Williams, the 21-year-old stepping across in the 12th minute and diving on a Brent Sherwin grubber in the 49th for his two tries. He twice stretched his right arm out towards the tryline, but his first effort in the second

minute hovered above grass before he was pulled back and his second in the 33rd was controversially ruled short of the chalk by video ref Chris Ward. Williams was eventually rested in the 73rd minute and received a standing ovation from the blue and white army.'

Folkes was hugely impressed. 'I don't know what he could do to play much better than that tonight,' said the coach. 'He was pretty dominant for most of the game.'

The Roosters' captain Craig Fitzgibbon agreed, saying the opposition barely stands a chance when the young second-rower is in such dominant form. He said playing SBW was now more about containment because it was virtually impossible to stop him. 'Playing against him like that I suppose I don't know if you can stop him — it's just a matter of minimizing

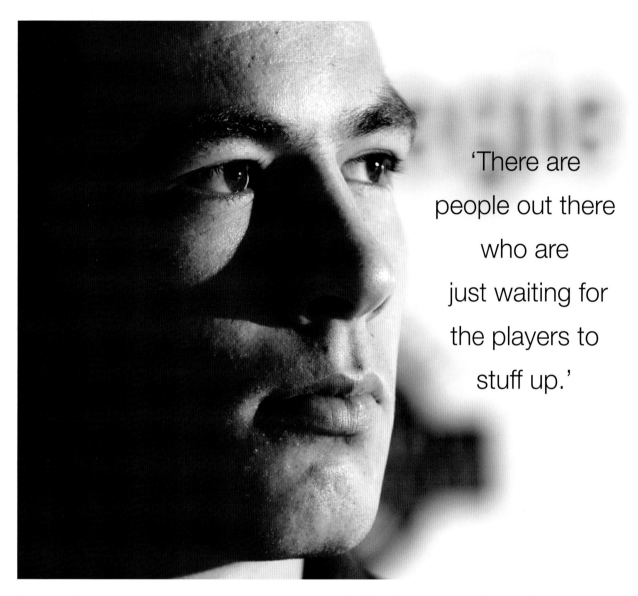

'There are people out there who are just waiting for the players to stuff up.'

him,' Fitzgibbon said. 'He is going to get you at some stage. He is just that good.'

By season end he topped the Bulldogs' try-scoring charts with his 14. The jibes about his habit of injury had been dispelled with 21 games in the season and a total of 1351 minutes logged. He'd topped the hit-up count with 318. He produced the most offloads with an impressive total of 61 — an average of three per game. Somehow he bettered his performance against the Roosters in Round 22 against Canberra when he singlehandedly ripped the Raiders apart. He scored three tries and knocked Michael Dobson into last year with a bone-crunching shoulder charge. Williams led almost every statistic before he was replaced in the sixtieth minute to a standing ovation. He ended the afternoon with 23 tackles, three line-breaks, three offloads, 10 hit-ups and 145 m gained.

Graham Lowe — one of the most astute judges of rugby league talent after coaching success in New Zealand, Australia and England — had been wowed as well. 'He has been nothing short of astounding, such is his offloading and playmaking skills,' he wrote in the *New Zealand Herald*. 'I asked myself again: "Is he the greatest I have seen?" The pendulum has moved further to confirming it — "probably" is where I'm now at.'

BREAKING OUT

THERE'S a joke about Khoder Nasser, the manager of Anthony Mundine and in 2008, for the first time, of Sonny Bill Williams. It goes something like this: NRL boss David Gallop is caught in a lift with three people: Osama bin Laden, Khoder Nasser and Adolf Hitler. Gallop has a gun, but only two bullets. What does he do? Shoots Khoder — twice!

Nasser is an easy target. Because Mundine — a three-time World Boxing Association Champion — is outspoken and controversial, Nasser has been cast as something of a puppet master by some in the Australian media. They blame him for encouraging Mundine's stances on everything from race, religion and rugby league instead of giving Nasser the kudos which should come for ensuring 'The Man' is a very rich man indeed.

When Nasser took over Williams's affairs, many in rugby league wondered how it would affect SBW's status. After all, Mundine — a former star with St George and Brisbane — had successfully made the transition to boxing under Nasser's guiding hand when he walked out on a $600,000-a-year deal with the Dragons in the late 1990s.

So the alarm bells rang loud and clear within the NRL in the middle of the 2008 season when Nasser made his first significant statement as Williams's manager.

It was 23 May and Nasser told the Australian media that Williams — who was in the first year of his new five-year deal with the Canterbury Bulldogs — could walk out on rugby league within two weeks. 'He has made a statement and if an [NZRU] offer was to come, he would definitely consider it,' Nasser said. 'He was basically saying he has achieved what is there to be achieved in league.' Williams wasn't happy at the Bulldogs, according to Nasser. 'These things are all going to come to a head soon,' he continued. 'We will have to work out what will happen; we are going to have to meet up with the club [the Bulldogs] in the next two to three weeks.'

What wasn't known at the time was that the great All Black captain Tana Umaga had already met with Williams, Nasser and Mundine. Umaga was the coach of the newly promoted French rugby first division outfit Toulon and had a $1-million-a-year offer on the table for Williams. He told Kiwis coach Stephen Kearney about his plans, but Kearney — who had planned to pick Williams in his World Cup squad later in the year — was powerless to stop Umaga's advances. 'Tana was up front with me. He said: "I've spoken to Sonny's management group", and he made sure to keep me in the loop of what was going on. I was certainly aware of his interest in Sonny and he was here doing the sly. I made Tana aware of what the plans were for Sonny, not only for the World Cup but also our game in New Zealand. [But] who am I to step in and interfere? What I can tell you is Tana did tell me that he and Sonny had been communicating.'

Williams was, it turns out, ripe for the taking. He was unhappy with his earning potential being limited by a salary cap — he was earning $400,000 a season — and felt under-appreciated by the Bulldogs management. And he was 'over' the constant newspaper coverage of his personal life and was unhappy with the choice of coach to take over at the end of the 2008 season, Kevin Moore.

Still, after Nasser's 23 May statement, when the Toulon deal remained unsigned Williams reaffirmed his commitment to the Bulldogs during a three-hour meeting with club officials, where he also expressed his captaincy aspirations, but deep down he remained unhappy. Indeed, he would, a year later, reveal the extent of those frustrations when interviewed by the *Sydney Morning Herald*'s Brad Walter. He talked of how his controversial deal came about and the chaos behind the scenes as he prepared to become a virtual international fugitive after breaking a contract with the Bulldogs that had four years left to run.

'It all just happened so quickly,' Williams said. 'It was pretty much just a week before I left that I knew I was going. The contract came through in French and they basically said, "Sign this now, cuzzy." That was when I took Tana's word for it. I said, "Bro, are you sure this is legit?" and he said, "Yeah", and that was it. I just signed it. The whole thing only took about five or 10 minutes but straightaway I knew I had made the right decision.

'When I signed that contract and faxed it through to France I just sat there feeling so relieved and thinking "f—" ... But I was just so happy. At the end of the day I said to Khoder I would play for nothing just to get out. That was how strongly I felt about it. I didn't even care if I got nothing.'

Eleven days later, on 26 July, Williams boarded a flight in Sydney that would take him to London via Singapore and eventually the south of France. 'When I hopped on that aeroplane it was like walking into the unknown, but walking into the unknown feeling that I was free — not that I was in prison or anything like that but that's just the way I felt. It didn't matter where I was going, it was just the fact I was getting out. I wasn't happy and I just thought, "I will take things into my own hands", but it wasn't until I started packing my bags that I realized this was it. I walked out the door and my girlfriend was crying but, looking back now, I know I made the right decision for me and my family because I am just so much better off financially, mentally and physically as well. I've got no regrets. If I did do it all over again there would be certain things I would change but I wouldn't change leaving.'

The critics rounded quickly on Williams and Nasser. 'Already guiding the career of one of the most disliked athletes in Australia, in Anthony Mundine, Nasser has recently taken charge of one of the most popular, Sonny Bill Williams,' wrote the *Daily Telegraph*'s Paul Kent, 'and within a few short months appears to be already leading him down the same road as Mundine. What Nasser is doing with Williams amounts to nothing short of high treason. A shameful bid to exploit Sonny Bill, a deliberate kick in the guts to rugby league.'

Another *Daily Telegraph* columnist Rebecca Wilson said Williams — or rather '$BW' — had 'no basic values' and was 'a disgraceful example of how greed is turning many of our footballers into mercenaries who don't care about anyone except the bloke in the mirror'.

Williams went underground in London as the battlefield in Australia took shape. On the one hand,

All Black great Tana Umaga enlisted the help of Kiwis coach Stephen Kearney as he masterminded the deal which would take Sonny Bill Williams from Sydney to Toulon.

Mundine, already a polarizing character in Australia, was talking on his mate's behalf. Mundine said Williams told him he'd 'done the right thing' and hoped to forge a successful career in rugby and potentially play for the All Blacks. 'He was unhappy and maybe he had new challenges, maybe the new challenge for him was to become an All Black,' Mundine said. 'He'd spoken to me about these things before so maybe he felt like he'd had enough of rugby league and that he had new challenges in rugby union and this was the first step.'

On the other hand, the Bulldogs and the NRL were preparing to take legal action against Williams in an effort to enforce the contract they had with the player as well as stop him from playing for Toulon. NRL boss David Gallop was on the front foot saying Williams's only hope of being accepted back into the rugby league community was to stay well away from French rugby union fields. 'I am really clear on this,' Gallop warned. 'If Sonny was to play rugby union in France in defiance of his contract, then like many people I believe the door should be closed on him returning. I was asked what our attitude would be if next week he came back and admitted he made a mistake.

Obviously, that is a completely different situation.'

Virtually as Gallop was speaking, the Canterbury club were confirming they would fast-track an injunction to prevent Williams from playing rugby. A copy of Williams's contract was leaked to the media and showed Sonny William Williams had signed and committed himself to the Bulldogs for five years on 16 May 2007, little more than a year before he walked out on the club in the most explosive of circumstances.

The contract was tendered to the New South Wales Supreme Court as part of the affidavit to stop Williams playing rugby in France. It revealed the guaranteed $2 million Williams would have earned along with the ability to inflate the amount with third-party sponsorships. The contract also contained a section in which Williams agreed to not 'participate in any football match of any code other than matches approved by the club and the NRL . . .' A further clause stated Williams agreed to 'not play the Game with any person, team or organization save for the club or in a Representative Match or matches in the Related Competitions except with the prior written consent of the Club'. As well as Williams, Nasser and Toulon president Mourad Boudjellal were added to the Bulldogs' lawsuit on the basis of them having engaged in inducing Williams to break his contract.

The Bulldogs' lawyers won the right to enforce the injunction, meaning Williams would be in contempt of court if he proceeded to play for Toulon. 'The evidence before the court satisfies that the first defendant (Williams) has failed to attend to his contractual responsibilities,' Justice Robert Austin told the parties. 'There is evidence he has entered into a contract with the second defendant (Toulon) ... and intends to play in a rugby match this evening.' Austin also acknowledged that the plaintiffs — the Bulldogs and the NRL — had proven Williams could be successfully sued for damages in New South Wales if he breached the order.

Within hours of the ruling it emerged that the Bulldogs would settle for a financial settlement from Williams to resolve the issue and when the player pulled out of a pre-season friendly, there was much goodwill from his former boss. 'It is a good sign for us,' Bulldogs CEO Todd Greenberg said. 'I suppose it's the first development that shows both Sonny Bill and Toulon have recognized that any order of the Supreme Court is not something that you can take lightly. It is a serious piece of legislation and he should act accordingly, which he has done and that's a pleasing sign. It's also important in that it shows you can't ignore it [the injunction], regardless of where you are in the world. It does have significant ramifications. So people who say that contracts aren't worth the piece of paper they're written on, I think this sends a very clear message that if you've got a contract and breach it, and the Supreme Court then has a look at that, then you've got some ramifications.'

Eventually, Mundine would provide Williams's route out of league and any civil action from the Bulldogs by paying the lion's share of $750,000 to the Canterbury-Bankstown club. '[He lent] not all of it, but a fair bit of it,' Williams would say in 2009. 'But I've been working hard at paying it back.'

Greenberg said the Bulldogs remained bitterly disappointed at the manner in which Williams had deserted his teammates and his supporters. 'We have, however, reached the point where we need to get on with business and we have withdrawn the injunction against him playing for any other club,' he said. 'Neither the Bulldogs nor Sonny Bill have anything further to gain by drawing this situation out any further. With this matter resolved we now look to finishing off our final few games of the season as strongly as possible and delivering [coach] Steve Folkes the farewell he deserves.'

Anthony Mundine — the former St George star and boxing champion — was a key figure in convincing Sonny Bill Williams to leave rugby league.

The rugby league community turned on Sonny Bill Williams in an instant when he walked out on his contract with Canterbury-Bankstown to sign with French rugby.

SONNY BILL WILLIAMS may not have been a rugby league player any more, but he'd lost none of his star quality when it came to the sporting world Down Under. His appearance on *The Footy Show* 12 days after leaving Australia was one of the most anticipated interviews on either side of the ditch in 2008. And with the rugby league world and many new curious rugby fans watching, SBW didn't disappoint.

His detractors tried to paint him as being under the spell of Khoder Nasser and Anthony Mundine. But it was clear Williams had made the decision by himself and for himself. Yes, he had asked for and received advice, but ultimately Williams was calling the shots. Indeed, Nasser — who was happy to mentor Williams — actually advised him to rethink his desire to work with him because he knew his reputation (and that of Mundine's) would have a negative effect on how some sections of Australia's media would cover him.

And it even transpired that Nasser, a devout Muslim, was unwittingly the subject of one of the final breaking points for Williams at the Canterbury club. He told *The*

Footy Show from his base in France that one of the final straws was when Bulldogs coach Steve Folkes approached him at training earlier in the year about newspaper reports he was becoming a Muslim. 'I rock up to training and Folkesy, Steve Folkes, someone that, to be honest, has never paid any interest in my personal life, he comes up to me and starts saying, "You're not turning Muslim, are you?" I just laughed. I said, "Seriously, you're joking", and then he has a go at Anthony: "You're kidding yourself if you're taking advice off him." I [started] to think, "Who is he to question my friends?"'

He also addressed the subject of money and how he hoped his actions would have a positive spin-off for the NRL players he'd left behind. 'If a lawyer, if a teacher, if a bus driver, if they're on $40,000 and they get offered a lot more to go somewhere else, what do you think they're going to do? Are they going to change bus companies? Or are they going to sit there and say, "All these people want me to stay here because I'm the best bus driver in the jurisdiction,

There was plenty on the mind of Sonny Bill Williams as he contemplated the press storm he left behind him when he turned his back on rugby league.

blah, blah, blah." It's just common sense.

'Hopefully, some good can come out of what I've done and it wakes everybody up and they realize that something needs to be done. What I've done, it has shown it's just not about me, it's about the boys getting a fair go, you know what I mean? It's about them having the balls to stand up for themselves, and get what they should be getting. Because if we're going to be treated like that, why can't we treat the clubs like that? I just want to see the game and

the players looked after the way they should be because the crowds don't turn up to watch [NRL CEO] David Gallop play . . . they turn up to watch the players play. When I think about it, David Gallop, you know, he has got a lot of problems, rather than me. He shouldn't be worrying too much about me, he should be worried about looking after these new boys because I'm telling you, things aren't going too well over there at the moment.'

Williams also explained the pull of Umaga — a one-time Junior Kiwi before his rise through the rugby ranks with Wellington and the Hurricanes and then graduating to being the first Samoan skipper of the All Blacks. 'Ex-rugby league player, rugby league convert, All Black captain, Samoan heritage, icon of the game. It sums it up really,' Williams said. 'I'm with an icon, Tana Umaga, who I really think I can learn a lot from, and I want to play for the All Blacks one day, so that keeps me motivated. One day I want to be the best centre, because that's the position I want to play. I want to be the best centre in the world. But I've got a lot of hard work and a lot of things I need to accomplish before then. I've got to be very dedicated, and like I said, [put in] a lot of hard work.'

Here are some edited extracts from Williams's interview on *The Footy Show*. Williams was asked about how his former teammates — including Andy Ryan — had been upset at him walking out.

> **SBW:** I'm just a bit hurt that some of the players have come out and bagged me straightaway without knowing the facts, because I thought with them knowing the kind of bloke I was, there would have been a legitimate reason for me doing what I've done. At the end of the day, those players that have stood up and hammered me straightaway probably weren't my friends in the first place.

Did he understand their anger?

> **SBW:** I never like seeing my close mates losing like that, but these boys know that what I've done is not just about me, it's about the young boys coming through . . . hopefully these players start getting treated a bit better, not just like cattle.

What did he want to say to the fans?

> **SBW:** I would like to think that one day, these young kids who've got the Sonny Bill jersey, or my poster on the wall, that they grow up and they realize that what I've done is not just about me, it's about everyone. It's about all the players. I just hope they just do realize that one day.

What did he think about being called a coward?

> **SBW:** What did I do? I stood up, I stood up for myself, for what I believe in. I stood up for all those other players that are sitting at home. Do you think before I left I didn't think my name was going to get slammed, that I wasn't going to get vilified, that my family weren't going to get harassed . . .? What I took, it's not a coward act, it's a ballsy act.

'I'm no coward, you know. I stood up for myself and I stood up for player rights.'

Journalists went searching for players to criticize Williams's appearance and message. Australian skipper Darren Lockyer was critical but not scathing. 'He sounds like he is confused,' the Brisbane icon said. 'He is a man now but he still seems like a kid. He just seems confused and whether these people around him are misdirecting him or not, I don't know.'

Roosters captain Craig Fitzgibbon agreed there was some dissatisfaction among players about how much they earn in comparison with other codes but questioned SBW's loyalty. 'In some respects he has got a point but I wouldn't do that to my teammates, to the fans. We're not trying to say we're doing it tough or we've got no money or we're broke, everyone is trying to say they want their worth in a rough comparison to what other codes are getting. But what [Williams] has missed is, "I love my club, I love the colours I wear". And, "I wouldn't do that to my teammates, I wouldn't do it to the fans and I wouldn't do it to the game that has given me so much".'

And Steve Price — Williams's skipper when they won a Grand Final together in 2004 — offered this sobering thought. 'If you had asked 10 weeks ago, "How will Sonny Bill Williams leave the game of rugby league?" most would have said as a superstar ... I don't know whether that's the case now.'

WHILE rugby league was struggling to deal with the departure from their ranks of Sonny Bill Williams, the man himself was having no trouble embracing his new career path. He was on a mission, with the endgame being the dream of playing for the All Blacks at the 2011 World Cup in New Zealand.

And Williams wasted no time in impressing his new teammates at Toulon with his work ethic and desire to learn. Coach Tana Umaga, with a pre-season game against Carqueiranne-Hyères looming, enlisted the

Sonny Bill Williams in his Toulon strip — in this game playing against Clermont.

help of his former All Blacks colleague Jerry Collins and one-time Auckland Blues and Crusaders star Orene Ai'i to help SBW with his transition.

'Tana just asked a couple of us to help him out,' Ai'i said. 'Being the player he is and the sort of guy he is, he's always willing to ask questions. Sonny will be the first one to say that he's got a lot of ground to make up. He's got to learn but he'll pick it up real quick. It will be amazing how much he improves over the next week. We're all going to pitch in and help him out as much as we can.' Ai'i said Williams had spent his first session 'just asking where he had to be at certain times at defence and on attack as well. It's just the basics really, trying to get his head around the moves and the lines. He'll have no problem running the lines; he's just got to get the names and the calls in his head. You can see, once he's got the ball in his hands that's all he really wants.'

Anthony Mundine, who was in France with Williams as he found his feet, was obviously confident Toulon has signed a physical specimen like no other. 'Certain athletes just have such ability that they can cross codes or sports,' he told *Sunday News*. 'Sonny is one of those. He has exceptional hand–eye coordination and his work ethic, determination, desire and ambition are huge. Whatever he wants to do, he can. Not in the rugby league or rugby union circles can I say I've ever seen anybody of his stature or with his skills and drive to be the best. I've yet to see anyone match that, so he's a pioneer in that sense.'

Certainly, when he appeared in Toulon's colours for the first time the ball was what he was demanding. And when he had it he made his mark against Carqueiranne-Hyères with a series of explosive bursts. In one run, he palmed off an opponent with ease and sent a teammate dashing towards the tryline. His debut was set to be a resounding success, until his crunching trademark rugby league shoulder charge left his French opponent Laussucq Arnaud on the ground for several minutes and Williams in the sin-bin.

Arnaud told the *Daily Telegraph* he felt like he had been 'electrocuted' in the illegal tackle. After recovering, he was well enough to joke that he was the league convert's 'first victim' and would be seeking compensation. 'I want his socks and his shorts and then I'll forgive him,' Arnaud said.

Toulon's billionaire president Mourad Boudjellal conceded that his star recruit would take time to adapt to the new code. 'He's obviously in the process of learning the differences in rugby union and rugby league,' he said after watching his charges storm to a 50–5 win. 'Bit by bit he'll pick them up. Rugby league is perhaps more aggressive than union. When he came to centre he got a bit more ball. Tonight, the Toulon public have discovered an amazing player who is going to play for us in [the French first division]. The two or three balls he did get, he showed great enthusiasm. The supporters really appreciated that and we're hoping to get a lot more from him.'

Three weeks and a lot of tutoring later, Williams made his first-class debut for Toulon in France's Top 14 championship. In the opening game of the season the former leaguie was the star turn as they defeated top-ranked Clermont 22–16. And to rub salt into the media on hand hoping to report on his struggles, Williams scored a try.

His progress was halted soon afterwards when he cracked a fibula in his leg in the game against Brive. Many in the Australian media screamed 'karma' as they recounted stories about his injury record at the Bulldogs where Williams missed 47 games from a possible 120, through injury. He had shoulder reconstructions, ankle injuries, knee injuries, bruised bones, more ankle injuries, and stress fractures. In both feet.

But the injury would prove to be a silver lining because on the other side of the world John O'Neill — the Australian Rugby Union's shrewd boss — was monitoring the ongoing interest from Australia in the New Zealander playing club rugby in France. The Wallabies were set to play against the Barbarians in

'Not in the rugby league or rugby union
circles can I say I've ever seen
anybody of his stature or with
his skills and drive to be the best.'

the middle of the following year to kick-start their 2009 domestic test programme. The game was scheduled for the same week as State of Origin I and was set to be lost in the enormous coverage and publicity which goes with any league game between New South Wales and Queensland.

O'Neill, though, knew the Barbarians club had a tradition of picking one uncapped player when they play test opposition and O'Neill suspected that having Williams on board would ensure, for the week leading up to the game, that rugby union and not rugby league would be dominant in Sydney's frenzied media wars.

'Will he put bums on seats? I suspect he will,' O'Neill said when he eventually announced Williams had been secured for the showpiece event. 'Would I be happy about that? Yes, I would. We weren't involved whatsoever in his defection. It happened and it's been settled legally, and he's free to play. We're keen to see him play, and if he adds to the lustre, so be it.'

O'Neill didn't have to wait long for the biff to start in pro-league media. The day after the announcement of Williams's involvement, two great league identities, Tommy Raudonikis and Steve 'Blocker' Roach, were calling for the game to be boycotted.

'It's an absolute disgrace,' Raudonikis told the *Daily Telegraph*. 'He shouldn't even be allowed back in the country. They should send him straight back to New Zealand. I can't forget what he did to the Bulldogs. It was dreadful and unsporting. No one should go to the game. All Sydney sports fans should boycott the event. I reckon it's just a publicity stunt because the match is only three days after Origin I. I just don't rate Williams as a person. I would hate to be alongside this bloke in the trenches.' Roach added: 'Only his family will go to the match — he has duded everyone else. People won't forget how he left the Bulldogs.'

Wallabies legend Simon Poidevin fired up the following day, describing the boycott call as dumb. 'The more they call for a boycott, the more people will turn up,' Poidevin said. 'That is dumb in capital letters. Blocker and Tommy should take their small-

world glasses off and start to realize that a sportsman in Sonny Bill's position can play anywhere he likes in the world.'

Williams's manager Khoder Nasser and Mundine had, like O'Neill, been planning, too. That was obvious when it was subsequently announced that, 11 days before the game for the Barbarians in Sydney, Williams would make his professional boxing debut in Brisbane, on the undercard of Mundine's *KO to Drugs* headlining IBO middleweight world title bout with fellow Australian Daniel Geale.

'I said to [Mundine] that I didn't want this to be a charity fight, I want it to be serious,' Williams said. 'I believe strongly in the *KO to Drugs* cause so I want to do it properly. With it being here in Australia I knew there would be a lot of scrutiny of me and I thought this was a good way to turn that into something positive. I'm still rusty as a boxer, but I want to give it my best crack.'

Williams had spent six weeks training in a Toulon boxing gym before he arrived in Australia for his final preparations, which included an open sparring session with local heavyweight Alex Leapai. Said Mundine: 'I want to make sure my brother is prepared the best he can be in such a short time. People have got to understand that this is his first fight and Sonny is fighting a bloke on an even keel ... but he has come a long way since he threw his first punch five or six weeks ago. This was supposed to be a basic workout today and he said, "No, let's pick it up, I want to get serious, after the second round." Alex is a well-known heavyweight and Sonny held his own.'

Tellingly, though, the sparring session would be tougher than his fight at the Brisbane Entertainment Centre. The 'opponent' — and this writer uses that term loosely for this occasion — was Kiwi bum Gary Gurr and SBW disposed of him early in the second round. Gurr had been dazed by a big uppercut in the first round and never laid a hand on Williams. For the purists on hand it was all nonsense, but it was a pro fight and it was a win. And for Williams that was

all that mattered. 'It was a whole new sport but it was fun, the lungs started blowing a bit hard. It was pretty tough out there, the way this guy was talking during the week I had to be on top of my game or I was going to get knocked out.'

If Williams didn't suffer a battering from Gurr, he certainly took his fair share of shots on his arrival in Sydney for the rugby game against the Wallabies. Only a year earlier he had been described as 'the most hated man in Australia' after his defection to rugby one year into his five-year deal with the Bulldogs. It was referred to often as a 'dog act' by many in Sydney's media and, a year on, they weren't about to let up on the 'Frog Dog'.

He was an easy target — case in point an article opening from the *Sun-Herald*'s Will Swanton penned before the announcement of the Barbarians selection: 'For every boofhead in the NRL, there's an army of good men,' wrote Swanton. 'For every "traitor" such as Sonny Bill Williams, there's a traditionalist such as Brett Kimmorley. When he did a runner from the Bulldogs yesterday, there was no need for club officials to check the departure lounge at Sydney Airport for clandestine France-bound rugby defectors. Kimmorley was merely taking his daughter to school ...'

An obvious calling point for journalists before SBW's arrival in Sydney was Canterbury-Bankstown Rugby League Club. The club's champion fullback Luke Patten was asked if he'd forgiven Williams. 'That's a really hard question for me to answer,' he said. 'I haven't had any contact with him since the day he left. Time does heal things, but … I've thought about this a fair bit, you know. I can understand that in football you have to do the best you can for yourself as a player. But I still think the way he went about it was wrong. He could have held off until the end of the year before he went and did that to us. But what do you do, eh? It's done now. He's gone, he's been gone for a long time and I think we've proved we don't need him back.'

A year earlier Patten had accused Williams of treachery after the Bulldogs failed to win a game following SBW's exit in round 17 and ended up claiming the NRL's wooden spoon. Now, with Williams due in Sydney and the Bulldogs riding along sweetly in first place, was there a chance of a peace-pipe being offered to the former star? 'I don't know, I really don't know. I'm sure it's going to get brought up a lot when he does get back to Sydney. It's still just a really tough thing for me to get my head around, especially the way I am with these kinds of things. The club means a lot to me and I'm very big on loyalty. Life has gone on, as we've seen this year. We said at the time the club was bigger than one player and we were right.'

Once back in Sydney, Williams chose *The Footy Show* to offer his apology — 299 days after walking out on the Bulldogs. 'I was angry at the reaction of a lot of people who were treating me like a mass murderer. It wasn't the way I wanted it to go down. I've thought about it for a while and am a bit upset with myself for not apologising to the boys. I didn't ring them and if I had my time over again I would have rung every player. I let the boys down by my actions. At the time I didn't ring because I knew how passionate the players were about the club and didn't think they would understand. Things were better left unsaid. But now I definitely want to change that and want to apologize to the fans, especially the younger ones who look up to me. I'm sorry for all the heartache I caused. Even though I had to pay $750,000 to get out of my contract, I've got no animosity towards the Dogs. They will always be my team. I've got the Bulldogs tattooed on my arm and I still cherish the memories that I have of playing for the club. I had some really good times there, so I wish them all the best and I still go for them.'

Williams also opened up about his life in France and his joy at being away from the media spotlight in Sydney. 'It's just good to be able to live a normal life over there,' Williams told the *Sydney Morning Herald*. 'It's not as crazy as it is here. It is totally, totally the opposite of being in Sydney. I'm so happy I made the move and I don't think I'll be looking back because I am just so much better off. There were times, especially when I got injured, that I did doubt myself and think "What am I doing?", but I never at any stage thought "I am getting on the plane and I'm going back." I never at one stage regretted it enough to say "That's it, I'm out."'

While Williams was winning over many with his honesty, the real reason for the trip home was upon him — a date with Stirling Mortlock at the Sydney Football Stadium. Finally, rugby fans Down Under were going to be able to judge for themselves whether Williams was worth pursuit from either the Australian or New Zealand rugby unions.

The Wallabies skipper admitted that he had been approached by a few people during the build-up to the game asking him to show up SBW. 'Yes, I've had a few people come up to me, and say, "Put a shot in for me," but it's all a bit tongue in cheek,' Mortlock said. 'Sonny Bill is a world-class athlete. He has proven his worth in league and is going very well overseas in union. Last week he was in the boxing ring, doing a bit of damage there as well. I've got no doubt he will be looking forward to playing on a bigger rugby stage and he will be up for it.'

Williams — the only Barbarians player not to have played test rugby — was thrilled to be surrounded by some of the most famous names in the game. After a season in Toulon where he'd helped them finish ninth and avoid relegation, he was set to star alongside the likes of England fullback Josh Lewsey, the Wallabies' veteran flanker Phil Waugh and former All Blacks Chris Jack, Jerry Collins and Justin Marshall.

'I've still got a lot to learn, but not many players can say they have played with the Barbarians, so it's an honour to be playing a game like this, especially with some of the names in the side,' Williams told the *Herald*. 'I just want to test the waters and see where I'm at, and with such quality players in the team all I need to concentrate on is what I've got to do, so that makes it easier for me coming into a big game like this. A lot of the blokes in this team have been around for a

'Sonny Bill is a world-class athlete. He has proven his worth in league and is going very well overseas in union.'

long time, they are all professionals and know exactly what has to be done, so I've been getting a lot out of watching them at training and listening to things they say. It's a bit of an eye-opener as to how they tend to play back here. It's a lot more free-flowing, even at training, and especially with the Barbarians' approach to how they play. I'm really looking forward to going out there and playing some running rugby. Over in France, unless it's a nice sunny day, we don't throw the ball around as much as I think that we could.

'You see the names like Stirling Mortlock, Matt Giteau and that gets you a bit nervous,' Williams added. 'And I want to show in this match that I'm not just a league player trying to play rugby, but that I'm a rugby player. I'm especially looking forward to playing against Stirling Mortlock. I've watched him since I've started playing league and I've really admired the way he plays not just with the ball, but also without the ball. He can hit really well. I'm not going to say I will go out there and be a star player or anything like that. I'm going to go out there and try to do the basics well, and not let Stirling Mortlock run through me.'

Collins — a teammate of Williams at Toulon at the time — knew better than anyone what to expect from the former Bulldog. And before the game he gave a hint of what would eventuate when he asked the media to show some patience before judging Sonny Bill Williams, rugby player.

'He is up to it,' Collins said. 'He wouldn't get invited to come and play [for the Barbarians] if he wasn't; if the club didn't think he was up to it. I've played with the guy, he should be fine. He's only been playing [rugby] for seven months ... hopefully he will play for longer than that. You guys [in the media] have just got to lay off him. You are asking a guy who has played for seven months to come and play like a veteran. He will go good if we play well. He is a great specimen of an athlete. Anyone who is an athlete can pick up things. He has that kind of gift that you can't teach — timing. But in terms of rugby union, he is still learning the game and will get better with time.'

Time was something he didn't have when Mortlock provided a rib-rattling 'welcome to the SFS' tackle early in the game. It brought the 39,688-strong crowd to their feet (Raudonikis and Roach's call for a boycott having fallen on deaf ears). Then Wallaby wing Lachie Turner got in on the act, too, with a hefty tackle. Williams had gone to Sydney to learn — and he was learning as the Wallabies cruised to a 55–7 win.

'After 10 months this is where I am at. I know I did some good things in the game and I did some bad things,' Williams said. 'I'm not happy with the way I played but I can sit back with a smile knowing that I can mix it with these guys. Australia are definitely one of the best teams in the world and when you watch it on TV you think "Wow, that's quick," but I now know that if I did come back here I could handle it and I know what parts of my game I need to improve on. I am going to have my critics and they are going to come out and bag me, but there is definitely a lot of improvement in my game and hopefully in another 10 months you will see a different player.'

While some of the Aussie media's reaction was harsh — 'Sonny Who?' said the *Sun-Herald*'s back-page headline while the *Sunday Telegraph* went with 'Baa-Baa Black Sheep — but what a waste of Sonny Bill's talent' — one of Williams's Barbarians teammates was impressed enough with what he saw to urge his employers at the NZRU to 'break the bank' to sign Williams ahead of the 2011 World Cup. 'He's still new to the game and to perform like he did, his strength and his size are going to get him through, no matter what,' said Luke McAlister whom the NZRU had prised back from Sale in the UK in 2009. 'Just a bit of guidance and a bit of skill work, and learning the game playing with good players, he'll be outstanding. I don't know what his plans are for the next few years, but New Zealand should break the bank to get him over.'

Another person who held a similar opinion was Fairfax's rugby doyen Spiro Zavos. He's been writing aboutrugby since 1979 and, like McAlister, he saw

enough at the Sydney Football Stadium to urge the NZRU to make their move.

'The first touch by Williams was almost fairytale stuff,' he wrote in his match report. 'He cut in and burst past Stirling Mortlock. The crowd roared as it seemed certain he was going to score. He took a couple of paces further to the inside and set himself to plant the ball over the tryline. At that moment he was smacked by Luke Burgess coming across in cover. Further Wallabies piled in. Williams was able to unload a pass but the opportunity to score was lost with some fumbling and poor passing to an unmarked winger.'

Zavos noted that in a rugby league match Williams would have scored. 'League people will hate hearing this but tryline defence in union is tougher than in league. In league it is a matter of breaking the first line. Williams did this. But in union you generally have to cope with a second and third defensive line coming across in cover. It was this second line that nailed Williams. He has played only 14 matches of rugby union and he will learn that the best option next time after he has made the cut is to veer out where the defence is more exposed.

'He has a lot of learning to do, clearly, as rugby union is a complex game and outside-centre is an extremely difficult position to master. Perhaps he would be better off playing on the wing in the Jonah Lomu manner. But he showed enough with his terrific physique, offloads, tackles and breaks that he has the ability to be a very good, and possibly great, rugby union player. Luke McAlister, who saw on the ground what Williams was capable of doing, told the NZRU to sign him up and pay whatever has to be paid to get him into an All Blacks jersey. If the NZRU doesn't

PREVIOUS PAGE: Sonny Bill Williams in his debut game for the Barbarians against Australia in Sydney in 2009; and he returns the favour (right) by getting hold of Wallabies No. 12 Matt Giteau.

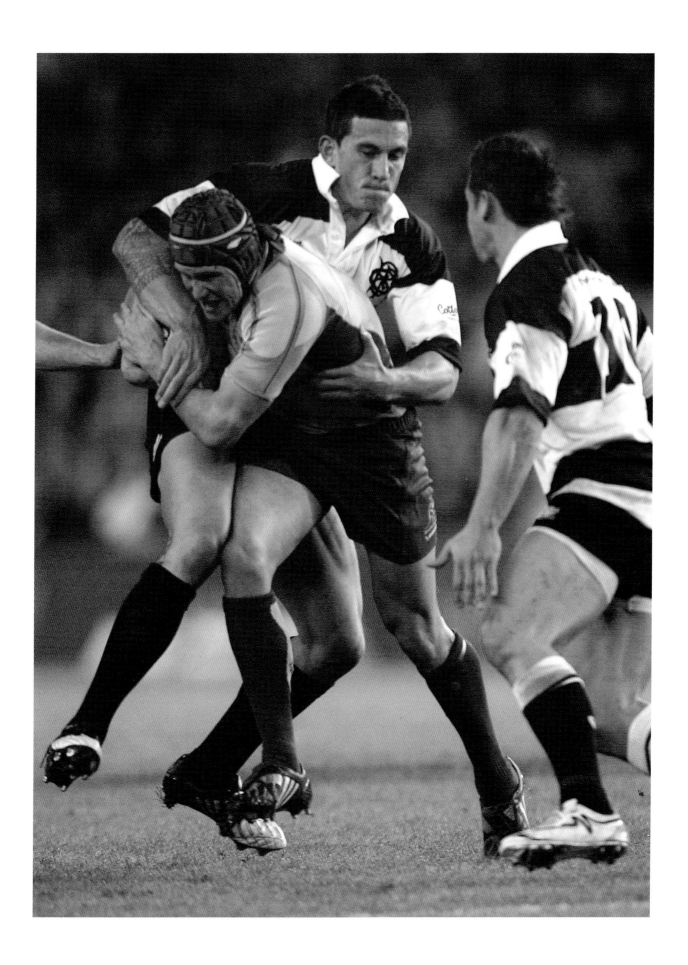

Sonny Bill Williams gets hold of Wallabies wing Drew Mitchell during the Barbarians game against the Wallabies in Sydney — his first rugby game in Australia.

make him an offer he can't refuse, the ARU, as it did with Robbie Deans, will.'

Williams revealed he was thinking about the possibility of a move to New Zealand after his next season with Toulon came to a close in the middle of 2010, but he was humble enough not to expect the All Blacks to make a move for him until he'd make dramatic improvements.

'When I first went to rugby I wanted it all, and I still do want it all because I am very driven, but I've realized that the idea of going back to New Zealand and trying to play for the All Blacks is not as much on the cards as I had first thought,' he told the *Sydney Morning Herald*. 'I'm enjoying my time in France. I just want to learn the game and to be considered a world-class rugby player. Wayne Smith did come over, that came out in the media, but he didn't come to see me. He actually came to see Daniel Carter [who was playing for Perpignan], and he was passing through Toulon at the time so we just had a coffee together. We just talked about a few things, and I told him I was signing with Toulon for another year, and we just discussed some different scenarios. In New Zealand, they have got a lot of depth and a lot of very good and very talented players in the position I am playing now so I think I am best to just worry about myself and do what's best for me. Whether that is staying in France or coming back to New Zealand, I don't know.'

While Williams was enjoying life in France, he admitted that playing in the Super rugby competition would have some appeal as he preferred watching it to the northern hemisphere version. 'You go through periods where it is just freezing for a couple of months and pissing down rain all the time so the rugby changes significantly. Then towards the end of the season when the weather improves it becomes more running football, and that's when I slimmed back down. Playing it when it's like that can get boring sometimes, and to tell the truth, I prefer to watch Super 14s than to watch a game over there because it's quick, ad lib rugby and it looks like they chuck the ball around a lot more. But they're the choices you make in life. Some people want to stay here to play for the Wallabies or play for the All Blacks. I think I'm a pretty confident player and I think over the next couple of years, if I stay on the field and I string together a lot of games and keep playing good footy and I keep learning the way I am now, I can. But at this stage, if I was a New Zealand selector, I wouldn't be in a rush to come knock on my door. You just have to look at the All Blacks backline and the players that are left out of the All Blacks team; you know the quality of the players over there is crazy.'

Part of the enjoyment of life in the south of France was the presence of his partner Genna Shaw. 'I have asked her to marry me but she's said no,' Williams told the *Daily Telegraph*. Shaw, 25, told him she was too young for marriage, but that wasn't deterring the then 23-year-old Williams. 'I didn't really get down on one knee but just in general talk. Hopefully, down the track — I know I am a lucky man.' Williams said he and his 'missus' were enjoying their relaxed lifestyle. 'I train in the morning then chill with Genna in the afternoon. There are lots of quiet beaches, we know all the spots. It is really cool.'

What else was cool was the reality that Williams had the option of playing for four countries — New Zealand (his place of birth), Samoa (through his father), France (through residency, if he remained there until 2011) and Australia. 'I have always just said I am half Kiwi, half Samoan, but I guess I am a bit Aussie,' Williams said. 'My grandmother is a full-blooded Australian. I think she grew up in Paddington. When I was young, it was funny because they always used to think my nana was a bit strange. It was just that Aussie sense of humour. And when I came over here I knew what she was on about. She's a good old lady.'

But, other than the French option, all others had to be put on hold as Williams had signed again with Toulon through to the end of the 2009–2010 season. The club's president Mourad Boudjellal and his new sporting director Philippe Saint-André had hoped to secure SBW on the three-year deal but Williams — just 14 games into his rugby career at that time — was determined to keep his options open because, unbeknown to them, SBW had received a call from All Blacks coach Graham Henry asking him what his thoughts were about coming back to try to make the All Blacks.

'I had a chat to him and he said to me that he'd like to play for the All Blacks but he'd only come back to New Zealand if he thought he was good enough,' Graham Henry recalled in 2010. 'He's that sort of person; he's very modest.'

CHASING THE
ALL BLACK DREAM

THE hunt was on. The All Blacks coaches had bookended Sonny Bill Williams in 2009. The team's backs coach Wayne Smith had met with him in France in March and the head honcho Graham Henry had telephoned him in November. They knew, after numerous conversations with Toulon's Tana Umaga — their former captain — that Williams was the perfect World Cup experiment.

But time was running out. Henry wanted SBW on the end-of-year tour to Hong Kong and Europe in 2010. With only four tests scheduled in 2011 ahead of the World Cup, the All Blacks coach knew it was imperative that if Williams was going to make a play for a place in his World Cup squad he had to be in the team that would contest a Grand Slam. For that to happen under the strict New Zealand Rugby Union rules, Williams would have to play a season of provincial rugby in 2010. It all meant that Williams needed to sign with the NZRU and head to New Zealand immediately after the French league came to

a conclusion in May — six months before the tour.

But how could the NZRU afford Williams? He was on a reported NZ$1.5 million a season at Toulon. And with his contract up at the end of the Top 14, offers were expected to come in from French and English rugby clubs and a long line of forgiving rugby league outfits in Australia.

How could the NZRU afford Williams? They didn't have to. They had the trump card, the ace up their sleeve — otherwise known as the All Blacks jersey.

IT was February 2010 when the NZRU finally conceded that they were after Sonny Bill Williams. CEO Steve Tew — strangely quiet when this reporter broke the story about Wayne Smith's clandestine meeting a year earlier — was now, finally, willing to go public with his organization's pursuit of the former league star.

'Clearly, he is a class athlete, and if he wants to come and play rugby in New Zealand and he is deadly serious about it, then we are open to some

very serious discussions,' Tew said. 'With these rugby league guys and the guys that are living overseas playing league or union, they really need to decide for themselves that they are going to do that so we can have a serious conversation. We obviously want to bring back any player who is genuinely interested in coming back and recommitting to a decent amount of time playing here. If they strengthen an All Blacks side leading into a World Cup then that would be clearly advantageous.

'All Blacks assistant coach Wayne Smith last year visited Williams in France, and the NZRU has continued to keep tabs on him. There are a number of people we talk to who are in that part of the world. This time last year, Wayne Smith spent quite a bit of time in Europe. He got around a lot of our UK-based players, and I caught up with Chris Masoe when he was back in New Zealand recently. He played in the French competition and he knows Sonny Bill and a number of the other guys who play in the French competition pretty well, and we had a conversation about how they were playing and the way they were going, so we've got a fair amount of information.'

Helping the All Blacks' cause was the strange decision from the Australian Rugby Union not to pursue Williams. The Wallabies high-performance director David Nucifora said that any suggestion the centre could pull on an Australian jumper in the 2011 World Cup was highly unlikely. 'We certainly wouldn't be out there chasing him. He's not on our radar,' said Nucifora, who a month earlier had declared the ARU's interest in another former league star playing in France, Mark Gasnier.

'Second-hand I have heard that he is eligible [to represent Australia], but that would all have to be checked out if we were approached by his management, and certainly no one has made any

All Blacks assistant coach Wayne Smith in discussion with Steve Hansen.

approaches to us at this point in time about him. It's just speculation, but we already have a lot of talent in that position. Look, it's not that he's unwanted or signing him is taboo. He's just not on our radar.'

Williams was, however, on the radar of at least two NRL clubs — the ambitious Newcastle club and the New Zealand Warriors. One sticking point, though, remained from Williams's less-than-perfect exit from Canterbury in 2008. Part of the settlement was an agreement with the Bulldogs that Williams would not be able to play for any other NRL club until the 2013 season — the year after his five-year Bulldogs contract was due to run out.

NRL chief executive David Gallop told Newcastle officials of the issue and said the NRL would support every effort to enforce the term. 'I did speak to one club during the week to point out to them that a part of the settlement between Sonny Bill Williams and the Bulldogs is a term that if [he returns] to the NRL he could only play for the Bulldogs before 2013,' Gallop said.

Jarryd Hayne — a superstar in the game thanks to exploits for the Parramatta Eels — was one of many NRL players that came out in support of the ban being lifted. He told the *Sydney Morning Herald*'s influential columnist Danny Weidler that it should be a no-brainer for Williams to return, and Hayne had support from some of the biggest names in the game, including Petro Civoniceva and Roy Asotasi.

Asked if the ban should be lifted by the NRL, Hayne said: 'One hundred per cent. David Gallop talks all the time about lifting the profile of the game. He'd be great for the game. It would be really silly, really stupid if they didn't allow him to come back into the game.'

Asotasi — the one-time Kiwis captain — backed Hayne in his support of SBW. 'I'd like to see the ban lifted and him back in the NRL and I reckon he's a much better league player than he is a union player.' And elder statesman Civoniceva thought it was time to forgive SBW. 'I think he's done his time, he's had a good holiday in France. It's been long enough. If he

wants to return to the game so be it.'

As the hype in the NRL built about Williams, the Warriors declared their interest in acquiring the player. 'Sonny Bill is a proven player at NRL level,' said CEO Wayne Scurrah. 'Commercially, he would be strong for a club like the Warriors in regards to bums on seats. We have to weigh up our options regarding recruitment but Sonny Bill would be attractive. If he was to return to the NRL, it would be a bit like Tiger Woods coming back to play golf.'

Another member of the Warriors front office, former skipper Dean Bell, knew securing Williams would go a long way to knocking rugby union off the front page of the local newspapers on a weekly basis. 'Let's not beat around the bush,' Bell told *The Australian*. 'It would be a massive boost not only for the club, but I also think the NRL. People don't sit on the fence with him — they either love or hate him. There's no denying the attraction of having a player like him back in the game. He's up there with the best athletes I have ever come across. It would have a tremendous impact on the profile of the game over here. It would be a massive coup, not only for the Warriors but for the New Zealand rugby league. We're in competition with [rugby union].

'Signing him is a long shot. We're not hearing anything one way or the other. I suppose it really comes down to what sort of guidance he's getting. When we bumped into him with the Kiwis for the Four Nations [in 2009], he came and visited us when we were in Toulouse — he seemed to miss that camaraderie he had with the rugby league group. He knows that we're interested and that's as far as we're going to go now. You don't put people in a corner. You express your interest and they have to want to come to you. There are a lot of things to overcome. I think it would be a good option for him to come to New Zealand where he would be away from the constant media attention and glare players are under in Australia. It's more laid-back here.'

Even Steve Price, who had been critical of Williams in

Warriors talisman Steve Price — and Sonny Bill Williams's former skipper at Canterbury-Bankstown — wanted SBW to sign with the Auckland NRL club instead of the NZRU.

2008, wanted his old Bulldogs teammate to make the trip across the Tasman to the club he had called home since 2005. 'We're talking about Sonny Bill Williams,' Price said. 'He's a New Zealand kid. Everyone knows his ability ... he does things no other player can do. For the game to get him back would be great.'

As it was, the Warriors' interest via Scurrah began a process which saw the Bulldogs — just as they did in 2008 — admit that if a rival club was prepared to pay them a substantial fee, they would allow Williams to play before the 2013 season.

'We had a brief discussion while we were both together at the CEOs' conference earlier in the week,' Todd Greenberg, Canterbury's boss, told Fairfax of his meeting with Scurrah. 'Wayne asked me to clarify our position on Sonny which was, in effect, quite simple. The terms of release between us and Sonny stipulate that he can't play for another NRL club until the 2013 season. I said to Wayne that if the Warriors were entertaining any thoughts of wanting him to play for them prior to that, he should give me a call and we will have a discussion then.'

Greenberg said he would be willing to have a 'commercial discussion' with any club about paying the Bulldogs for an early release. 'All I've said at this stage is that under the current terms another club wouldn't be able to sign him. But if someone wants to call me and have a commercial discussion, which effectively would involve some sort of payment for an early release, we would be happy to have that discussion.'

The Bulldogs' stance split rugby league. Canterbury's greatest-ever player, Steve Mortimer, reckoned that Williams should be forgiven for having walked out on Canterbury. 'I think he should be able to play [elsewhere] if the Dogs are compensated,' Mortimer said. 'I think what he did will be hurting Sonny more than anyone else. Hopefully, this has been a lesson in life for Sonny Bill. And I hope he has learnt from it. If he had hung in there and toughed it out, he would have got the rewards last year when the Bulldogs went so well. As I said, as long as the Bulldogs are paid, I would let him play. The door is always open.'

Canterbury fans made their thoughts known in a *Daily Telegraph* online poll with more than 75 per cent of respondents voting against allowing Williams back into the NRL. Bulldogs Army supporters club member Darren Barrett was also against seeing Williams sign with the Warriors. 'I want him to come back to the Bulldogs — but only if he apologized to the club, the fans, teammates and sponsors for doing his midnight run,' Barrett said. 'If he doesn't come here, then he shouldn't be allowed to go anywhere else. There was a lot of pain for Bulldogs fans when he walked out. When the going got tough, he simply said: "I've had enough." We weren't winning that year so he just left us.'

One man who hadn't given up on Williams was of course Toulon's billionaire owner Mourad Boudjellal.

He was determined to keep his star player in the south of France. Indeed, he was determined that if Williams was to play test rugby it would be for France. 'If the All Blacks want him and it does not worry them that he keeps playing at Toulon, I would not get in the way of him playing with the All Blacks,' Boudjellal said. 'But if he has to play in New Zealand to become an All Black and if he wants to be an All Black, he should go to New Zealand. That is certain. [But] in one or two years he could play for France. Voila!'

Boudjellal had been impressed by Williams's development and the impact he'd had at Toulon. 'He is a great player,' Boudjellal said. 'He is not yet at 100 per cent. He has a great potential. And we would like that potential to explode at Toulon.'

Tana Umaga — a former captain for Boudjellal's side — added to the speculation. He signed to play for Counties Manukau and suggested he'd be disappointed if his prodigy didn't follow him to the South Auckland union. 'I told him that if he does come back he had better play with me — I'd be disappointed if he didn't,' Umaga said. 'Everyone wants to know what he is doing. We have had a chat and all he wants to do is get his body right and get back on the field, which he is doing now. He has told his management to collect all the offers that come to the table and at the finish of the season he will decide. He doesn't want to do anything before that. That's the measure of the person. He just wants to prove himself, show what he has got and he is doing that brilliantly over here. We will just have to wait and see what happens at the end of the season.'

The Bulldogs, sensing that fellow NRL clubs had been scared off by their demands of an A$1 million pay-off to get them to allow Williams to play for a rival franchise, made it known that they would be prepared to consider alternative compensation. Ideas included Williams's new club shifting its first match against the Bulldogs to ANZ Stadium at Homebush and letting the home side take most of the gate. Other potential means of recompense also included sharing

profits from the increased membership, marketing, sponsorship and merchandising opportunities that gaining Williams's signature would provide.

By March there was confirmation from the Williams camp that a return to rugby league was indeed an option the player was taking seriously. And it came from a meeting between Williams's manager Khoder Nasser and Graham Richardson — the heavy-hitting Sydney businessman who had helped negotiate the final payout from the Bulldogs. They dined at a

When Tana Umaga signed for Counties Manukau in 2010 many suspected Sonny Bill Williams would follow him to New Zealand rugby via the South Auckland province.

Hurstville Chinese restaurant in Sydney — named, wait for it, Sunny's. 'Yeah I had lunch with Khoder and I will catch up with him and Sonny Bill when he is in Australia later in the year,' Richardson said. 'Just because we met up it doesn't mean that it's a given Sonny will be playing in the NRL. I do know that a return to the NRL is one of the things they are considering and I want to discuss his options with him. If I can help in the dealings he has, if he wants to return or otherwise, I will help out.'

As the speculation about his future grew by the day, Williams was doing nothing to discourage it. His form for Toulon was the best it had ever been. English rugby clubs had joined the race and a Japanese outfit had been in contact with Williams's representatives as well. Their desire to get Williams's signature only increased when he scored a try in Toulon's win against the Welsh side Scarlets. His performance prompted one Welsh media outlet to describe him as 'the most naturally gifted player in either code in the game at the moment'.

By April, Toulon were in first place in the Top 14 after beating former leaders Perpignan 33–23 — the team's eighth consecutive victory. The club's group of foreign players, which included Umaga, Williams, ex-Springbok Joe Van Niekerk, Australian Luke Rooney and English star Jonny Wilkinson, 'could no longer be called mercenaries', the French sporting newspaper L'Équipe claimed. 'They are as proud to wear the lily of the valley [the club's symbol] as any youngster from La Rade [the harbour], and with these globe trotters caught by the red and black passion [the team's colours], the club is scared of no one.'

'This was one of the best matches for a long time,' Boudjellal told L'Équipe. 'It has almost been 18 years since Toulon disappeared from the top. Today, we are back. I don't know if we are going to win, but I am going to work in the years to come, believe me. I have been perhaps the most highly criticized president of French rugby, but I have made a lot of financial and personal effort.'

Williams was to the fore again in Toulon's 26–23 win against Brive — an SBW try securing the win and booking a semifinal berth to boot. The performance inspired Sunday News' David Long to canvass several French-based rugby personalities who were effusive in their praise of the convert. They included New Zealander Vern Cotter, coach of the highly rated Clermont club, who said that in his debut year with Toulon Williams had looked like a 'league player playing rugby'. 'Now he looks like a rugby player playing rugby. It has taken him a little while to integrate into a role in 15-a-side rugby but he has enormous talent in line-breaks, offloads, power and speed. He is a remarkable sportsman and what I've seen over the last two years is that despite the injuries — which have stopped him playing consistently — his form and understanding have risen a lot over the last three months. Toulon have won their last [nine] games and he's been a big part of that. He's finally been able to stay on the paddock for a longer period of time and there's a lot more cohesion in the way he plays with his teammates now and that comes with the understanding.'

Cotter admitted he was as intrigued as anyone about the prospect of Williams playing for the All Blacks. 'You get a feeling that there's a maturity about the man, and that's part and parcel of his development. I feel he's on the right track. There's more cohesion about the way he plays, with regard to his teammates and the game plan. He's more adaptable now on the field. That was one of the issues he had last year — he was still trying to play rugby league in a 15-man game.

'He still had habits from league and it's taken him time to change those. Being in the environment he's in at the moment, in a team that's successful, has helped him, too, and as long as he sticks in teams like that he's always going to improve. If he's well coached and put into a team that's well structured and drives high performance from start to finish, he's someone who will bring something great. I think he's looking for that now. He's had a bit of a taste of performing in a team that's doing well.

'The big thing for him is that [signing with the NZRU] would be a challenge. Does he want the challenge? Well, that's a question only he can answer. I think it would be exciting for him as he's done very well in the 13-man game. Is he prepared to test himself in New Zealand? Personally, I'd like to see him do it. I'd like to see how far he can go — I'm as curious as the next person. I can see his raw quality and I have seen an improvement in his game, individually and collectively within the side. Putting him into an All Blacks framework and having the other players around him will be fascinating. Certainly, there is no doubt about his ability as a sportsperson. Athletically, he does some remarkable things on the paddock.'

Also in France, Pierre Villepreux — one of the more highly regarded rugby brains in France, first as a player, then club coach, then national coach — was the subject of a Peter FitzSimons' column in the *Sydney Morning Herald*. 'Last Saturday afternoon,' he wrote, 'I sat with [Pierre] as we watched Stade Francais take on Clermont, and asked him the obvious: if Mark Gasnier, the Stade Francais centre, was a Frenchman, would he make the French rugby side, which had just won the Six Nations Grand Slam? *'Probablement*,' he replied. And what about Sonny Bill Williams, who now plays for Toulon? *'Sans doubte.'* The translation? *Without doubt.*

Another to back Williams was the All Blacks great Grant Fox. As a first-five — a World Cup winning one at that — he knew about dealing with pressure and he was convinced Williams wouldn't be intimidated by the pressure that comes with playing top-level rugby in New Zealand.

'There will be a lot of pressure and expectation there, but Sonny Bill Williams is a high-performance athlete — he will put more pressure on himself than perhaps anyone, any outside influence, can,' Fox said. 'There is no way the NZRU would sign Sonny Bill on the basis of his marketing pull; they would only sign him if they believe in his potential as a rugby player. From the little bit I've seen of him I believe he would have the skill set to be very successful playing rugby union on a bigger stage than he is already. There is an element of risk in this, but I think it is a calculated risk. I can see him in the midfield simply because of his strength as a ball

All Blacks great Grant Fox — a World Cup winner in 1987 — had no doubt that Sonny Bill Williams could deal with the pressure of wearing the famous black jersey.

carrier. He can break the line and keep the ball alive in the tackle. He could also play at No. 6 or No. 8, provided he develops his work rate and his positional play as well. The midfield guys who are there in the All Blacks now will not want to give up their positions lightly and that competition would be healthy.'

A long line of All Blacks were also public in their support of the NZRU attempting to snare Williams. Brad Thorn — who successfully made the transition from life in the NRL with the Brisbane Broncos to the All Blacks — tipped a big future for Williams in union. 'I can't speak highly enough of him as an athlete,' Thorn said. 'Usually, you hear hype about a guy but they don't fulfil that. When I went back to league I thought he was every bit like the hype about him. He's an amazing athlete, he's probably an inch shorter than I am, about six foot four, his footwork ... he's an explosive, powerful, natural footballer. I think he'd go really well and it sounds like he's really starting to warm up over in Europe. It could be quite exciting to see him play.'

Dan Carter — the biggest name in All Blacks rugby — broke into a grin at the suggestion of combining with Williams for the Crusaders, who are in the running for his services for the 2011 Super 15 along with the Blues and Chiefs. 'If he plays in New Zealand it would be great to have him down there,' Carter said. 'He's a big man and it would be good to have him running off your shoulder every now and then. I haven't had a chance to see him play a full 80 [minutes], to be honest, but just looking at him, he looks like an athlete with real potential, so if they were to get him back that would be great. I've heard that he's played a lot better during his second year. It's obviously very tough to adjust, but he seems to be improving, which is good. He will only get better the more he plays.'

And Ma'a Nonu — the man whose All Blacks position Williams was after — was energized about the prospect of added competition for the No. 12 jersey. 'I think it's exciting,' Nonu said of Williams's desire to crack the All Blacks. 'There's that hype of someone else coming in. He's a megastar in league and played well for Toulon. I watched a lot of his games at Toulon and he was going well. He probably had the right guidance under Tana, who kind of helped me. So I think it's good for the game and good for me. But the All Blacks is a challenge in itself. When you get to my age, it's always a challenge and if you worry about it too much you get put off your game. If you look at New Zealand there are a lot of other second-fives who played well in the Super 14. So the reality is you have to play well all the time. Just because you played 12 for the All Blacks last year doesn't mean you will again this year. It's about delivering consistently.'

As for the man himself, Williams credited playing alongside Jonny Wilkinson — the England great — as the key to his rapid development. And he also believed

Dan Carter couldn't help but smile at the suggestion that Sonny Bill Williams could join him at the Crusaders for the 2011 season. Before that, though, the pair would be teammates for the All Blacks.

his understanding of the game had been fast-tracked by a brief stint in the forwards before Toulon coach Philippe Saint-André moved him to second-five where he played outside Wilkinson.

'After playing the game for a while you start to work out the position you like and for a while there I had a little stint in the forwards just to get more ball,' Williams told the *Sydney Morning Herald*. 'I hit up Philippe one day and said I wouldn't mind having a crack at No. 6 and he said, "No worries, why don't you train with the forwards?" So I did a couple of weeks' training with

'He probably had the right guidance
under Tana, who kind of helped me.
So I think it's good for the game and
good for me. But the All Blacks
is a challenge in itself.'

them and then he gave me 30 minutes one game. It was OK. I didn't mind it. I think more than anything when I went and trained with the forwards it helped me to understand the game a lot more and I really enjoyed it. You've got to remember that because I had never played before, when I came back from injury this season I had only played about 16 games of rugby and I was still trying to find my feet.

'But after that he put me in at second five-eighth and I really enjoyed that because I struck up a pretty good relationship with Jonny Wilkinson and I just found that the more I talked to him, the more confidence he had in me, so the more ball I got. Towards the end of the year it really paid off because we started to play some good rugby together.

'Philippe is a really good coach and he just told me to express myself and try to get as much ball as I could. I think that is why I had such a good season. I am just really enjoying playing rugby and after 30 or 40 games I feel like I have a lot more to learn. I think really knowing that I can put myself in positions where I can get a lot more pill and knowing when I can try and make a big hit ... I am really enjoying myself. I think maybe in the last three months or so it has started to feel like second nature and I was getting a lot more ball. I had never played rugby before so I needed to give myself a chance. It was tough at the start because last year they found I had been playing with compartment syndrome in my leg. It was weird because last year I was running around limping after 10 minutes or 20 minutes. It just didn't feel right. They misdiagnosed it. I went back at the start of the pre-season and they misdiagnosed it again. I just needed some time off and then when they found out what was wrong with it, it was the start of the season.

'Of course, when you are out injured there are a lot of things that go through your mind but I had only played about 16 games of rugby [the previous season] so I knew that if I could string another 15 or 16 games together, which I did, then I could assess it after that. I missed maybe 13 games but ended up playing

about 20 games and I was there for the good part of the season. I got to play in the Top 14 finals — that was a great experience.'

Wilkinson had no doubt Williams could make the transition to test football. 'I think he will go brilliantly. He was outstanding for Toulon and played really well. It was a real pleasure to play with him and a massive learning curve for me as well. His strength is his strength — his ability to keep the ball alive, his physicality, his ball movement and game awareness in space and people around him. I've not seen the likes of him before. Just watching the guy being able to ride tackles, even if it means sticking your arms in the air and being able to ride tackles in the ribs. He gets hurt, but never seems to go backwards.'

Williams's form, though, wasn't enough to inspire Toulon to the Top 14 title (they were eliminated in extra time by Clermont in the semifinal), but it did help the club reach the final of the second tier in the European Challenge Cup, where they lost to Cardiff 28–21. Despite the defeat, Williams claimed the man-of-the-match award. Boudjellal summed up Toulon's year with a classic French touch: 'Let's just say that this year we flirted, next year we are going to be sleeping with them because we hope to get two titles.'

Boudjellal, though, would have to attempt that feat without his star recruit who had just discovered a secret about his charismatic boss. 'For the whole time I was in France I thought he didn't speak English, but then after the last game he had a chat with me and spoke fluent English and talked about me staying with the club,' laughed Williams.

AN audience with Khoder Nasser is not a common occurrence. Sonny Bill Williams's manager normally doesn't engage the media unless he absolutely has

Tana Umaga played a big role in Sonny Bill Williams's rugby education in France, but so too did England great Jonny Wilkinson (right).

to. And, in that sense, he is a master manipulator of the fourth estate. If he needs to get a deal across the line and he thinks the press can help, he'll make sure his message gets out one way or the other. But when he arrived in New Zealand for a tour of the Super 14 franchises — courtesy of the NZRU — there was no need to call in a favour from a specific journalist or two.

'Sonny Bill loves Toulon,' Nasser said when he arrived in New Zealand. 'But we are talking about the No. 1 entity in world rugby, the New Zealand Rugby Union and the All Blacks, and I'm quite flattered to be invited.' The very public tour ensured a gaggle of journalists were camping out in the lobby of his hotel. And an extraordinary attack on Canterbury-Bankstown was a clear sign that Williams would not be playing in the NRL anytime soon, following the likes of rugby converts Mat Rogers, Lote Tuqiri, Timana Tahu and Mark Gasnier back to the NRL.

The battle for his signature was now a two-horse race. He was either going to be an All Black or be the cornerstone of Toulon's attack.

After a meeting with Graham Henry, Nasser said the Bulldogs' demands for financial compensation to release him from an arrangement whereby he cannot play for a rival team before 2013 had all but ended any chance of Williams returning to league. 'How can Sonny returning to the NRL be an option at the moment when you have got Canterbury — who didn't see the value in Sonny in the first place — thinking that another club should pay them to have Sonny's services?' Nasser said. 'They are having an impact on whether one of the greatest players to have ever played the game comes back because the man they hailed as the ground-breaking chief executive could never see the value in Sonny that the rest of the world could.'

Nasser also had the NRL in his firing line. 'Sonny is the NRL's No. 1 export but the Bulldogs are holding a gun to any club having him, and the NRL is a part of that. No other rugby league player has ever received what he has received or the media space or accolades he has, so he is actually the No. 1 propagator of the NRL because when people see Sonny play, they say, *Wow, where did he come from?'*

So there it was. It was now a battle between the NZRU and Mourad Boudjellal. Henry was offered some hope. 'We've had communication with Sonny Bill, and we've had communication with him through Khoder Nasser whom he respects a great deal. At the moment we're getting very positive reports about his rugby-playing ability in Europe. If it comes down to money we might get second. But if it comes down to the desire to play for his country ... that might clinch it.'

'THERE'S a lot to think about, bro.' Those were the words Sonny Bill Williams offered to the waiting press corps when he touched down in Sydney in May 2010 to prepare for his second professional fight on the undercard of Anthony Mundine's *KO to Drugs* event in Brisbane.

Clearly, he wasn't thinking about his opponent for the bout — Ryan 'Hulk' Hogan, who would have been more at home in a pantomime than a boxing ring. Either that or at a Denny's or KFC. More 'bulk' than 'hulk'. The fight would be over within 155 seconds. Williams, shaking his head, mouthed *Fuck me* at Hogan's pathetic capitulation before embarrassingly raising his arms in victory.

What was on his mind was the All Blacks. Khoder Nasser had returned from New Zealand singing the praises of the All Blacks coaches Graham Henry, Wayne Smith and Steve Hansen and the NZRU's boss Steve Tew. 'We put everything back to fit in those talks,' Nasser said of his meeting with Henry. 'We prioritized our meetings with the NZRU because they were extremely important. It's not every day that a person from anywhere can get a tour of New Zealand rugby by the No. 1 man in New Zealand rugby. It was extremely flattering. Graham Henry was a great host and just from the initial meetings and getting to know these people, they were very thorough. They know what they are doing and they know all good

'There's a
lot to think
about, bro.'

things take time and that there's a process.'

Nasser was convinced that if Williams turned his back on Toulon — and the riches they were offering — he would at least be going to a place where he would be given every opportunity to succeed.

Said Williams: 'I have said before that playing for the All Blacks is the dream of every young boy growing up in New Zealand, so it is something I have to weigh up. I am just thankful that they are interested. That is not to say I would go to New Zealand and just walk into the All Blacks. They are a very strong side with the calibre of players they have got, but I am always up for a challenge. Then again, I love Toulon, so we'll see. It's a nice place and a nice country. The lifestyle there is good, the people are really good, the coaching set-up is great and I think you could see in my rugby that I was enjoying myself there, so there is a lot to weigh up. If I go back to Toulon, I am pretty sure they won't just let me sign another one-year contract. They'll want me to stay there for a bit longer than that, so if I go back there it will be for a while.'

Williams said he needed to talk to Nasser before any decision would be made. 'I really trust in Khoder, I value his opinion so I will just sit down with him and work it out. That is what I have got him for. He can worry about that aspect of the rugby and I just worry about what happens on the field, because I am a big believer that if you go well on the field things fall into place and I thank God every day that in the last couple of months I have really started to understand and find my feet in rugby because those doors wouldn't be open right now.'

The NZRU — apart from offering Henry and Smith as taxi drivers during Nasser's time in New Zealand — were bending over backwards to get their man.

All Blacks coach Graham Henry (right) and his assistant Wayne Smith played a pivotal role in convincing Sonny Bill Williams's manager, Khoder Nasser, that the All Blacks were the right fit for the player.

So much so that the contract they offered Williams included a 'get-out clause' — in case he didn't settle in New Zealand and wanted to return to France. Acting NZRU chief executive Neil Sorensen told Fairfax his organization's offer 'extends to the end of 2012 but we have included opt-out clauses. We are trying to be as flexible as we can for Sonny. In an absolutely ideal world Sonny would play for a provincial union in the ITM Cup towards the end of July and then would be available for selection on the All Blacks' end-of-year tour. There is a lot of water to flow under that bridge. Sonny has a big decision to make. Hopefully, we will have an answer soon.' As a sweetener, Williams was also offered the chance to be a part of New Zealand's Sevens side at the Commonwealth Games in Delhi.

When Tew was back behind his CEO desk he was forced to defend the NZRU's pursuit of Williams. While they had proactively encouraged 2007 World Cup All Black Luke McAlister to return to New Zealand in 2009, the Williams sideshow was at a different level. Traditionalists were unhappy to see Henry driving Nasser around Auckland. Talkback callers complained that their relationship was already too 'cosy' — *How will Ma'a Nonu ever get selected again?* Others asked why they were pursuing him at all. *He'll walk out on the team as soon as he's unhappy ...* Another common theme was that the NZRU had no business trying to lure anyone to New Zealand. *If they want to play for the All Blacks they should come back to New Zealand off their own bat and start playing club rugby.*

Tew was having none of it. He denied suggestions Williams was getting a red-carpet-like treatment from Henry, and that the involvement of the All Blacks coach extended to anything on a contractual level. 'We have put a contractual offer in front of Sonny Bill, and it's been through the normal process of this organization,' said Tew. 'Graham — which is not unusual — has been involved in discussions to paint a broader picture for the player involved. We're talking to two or three other players in New Zealand contemplating their futures who might be important to the All Blacks, and they're also having discussions with the All Blacks coaches.

'There's no desperation. It indicates how professional we are, it indicates how much time and effort we're prepared to put into something we believe is worth doing properly, and that we don't do anything half-pie. Our coaches spend a lot of time with player agents; they just don't happen to have the profile of this particular guy. ... He certainly wasn't being a tour guide — he was just showing him what New Zealand rugby has to offer. We're talking about a high-profile player who has the potential to earn significantly more money playing almost anywhere else in the world, and we're trying to convince him this is a good place for his rugby. You'd expect us to be professional about it. This is a guy who's played professional football for a long period of time, he's played in the top provincial competition in Europe, has played for a team that's made the semifinals of the Top 14 in France. We're getting good reviews from people up there who have watched him play, we've watched a lot of his coverage, and he's being offered a contract [that reflects] someone who's played that kind of level in New Zealand or somewhere else.'

The French publication *Midi Olympique* reported that the NZRU offer was worth $NZ550,000. In contrast, Mourad Boudjellal had upped Toulon's offer to NZ$6 million over three years — believed to be the rugby world's richest-ever contract.

But on this occasion at least, money didn't talk because on 10 June Williams announced he had signed with the NZRU through to the end of the 2011 World Cup in a bid to achieve his dream of representing the All Blacks. 'I'm going to take up the opportunity to realize a dream and go back to New Zealand and try to aspire to play for the All Blacks,' Williams told *The Footy Show* in Australia. 'It's a lot less money than what Europe offers, but I just feel that for my immediate playing future this is the best decision for me.'

Despite having two seasons of rugby under his belt,

Williams didn't declare himself ready to represent the All Blacks. 'I wouldn't say I'm ready to. I'd love to; it would be a dream come true. But I feel that me putting myself in this position is the first step towards realizing a dream. I know there's fierce competition over there to play for the All Blacks and I've definitely got to go back and prove myself first and foremost, that's what first of all I'm looking to do. I'm definitely excited about … going to New Zealand and I'm just thankful to the New Zealand Rugby Union and Graham Henry and Wayne Smith. The All Blacks are the biggest sporting brand in the world and the chance to play for them in a competition that's watched by more than four billion people is something I couldn't let slip through my hands.'

Nasser moved quickly to have a crack at Williams's critics who had labelled him 'Money Bill Williams or '$BW' when he walked on out the Bulldogs. 'They've wasted plenty of their ink and time saying he's Money Bill Williams,' Nasser said. 'Now that he has knocked back a world-record offer, their silence has been deafening. What's their next line of attack going to be — that he is crazy for knocking back the money? What do they have to say now?'

The next decision to be made by the pair was where Williams would play his provincial and Super rugby. Hawke's Bay (in the Hurricanes boundaries), Auckland and North Harbour (both Blues) and Counties Manukau (Chiefs) had all made bids for him. But the favourites were always Canterbury and the Crusaders. A month or so earlier when Nasser had met with officials in Christchurch, he'd raved about the opportunity for his charge to play outside the All Blacks' 'conductor' Dan Carter — not to mention the province's other current All Blacks, which included skipper Richie McCaw, Brad Thorn, Kieran Read, Sam Whitelock, Owen Franks, Ben Franks and Andy Ellis. 'This is a great rugby franchise,' Nasser said following his visit to Canterbury rugby's HQ. 'You don't have a winning record of 83 per cent since 2004 for nothing. I have been impressed by their reputation

Who would have thought that this baby-faced Canterbury-Bankstown star (pictured here in 2004) would go on to be the most controversial figure in league and rugby before the decade was out?

FOLLOWING PAGES: Sonny Bill Williams playing his first game of rugby in New Zealand — for his club side Belfast.

and professionalism.'

When he was unveiled as a Canterbury and Crusaders player Williams admitted his 18-month contract with the NZRU carried plenty of risk, little security, and was a huge gamble. But it was what he wanted as he vowed never to sign another long-term contract. 'There's one line that has really stuck with me for a while now: *You're only useful as long as you are necessary,*' Williams told Fairfax. 'I wouldn't say I am a businessman. I would say I have become a lot smarter in the way I understand things. That line says it all. I guess sometimes it doesn't work both ways. I guess you could say I have grown up, matured. I have

seen a lot and I guess that probably sums it up.'

Asked about his NZRU deal, Williams explained: 'It's just about not getting locked into something. It's where I have a bit of power as well, not just the club. It gives me motivation and pressure on me to perform — if you don't, there's no contract. So it works both ways. It's the way I believe it should be. I have learned from my mistakes ... the business we are in is cut-throat. I have seen too many older blokes give their all for clubs then be told they are not wanted. Even blokes still on contract are told to look elsewhere. There is a reason why I am signing one- or two-year deals. I am 25 now, I am getting older, I've got to look out for myself and for my family as well as doing what's best for the club.

'Of course, if I don't make it, there will be mixed emotions. The pressure is on me. It's a gamble, but a gamble I am willing to take. I don't want to be 40 or 50 and say, "Yeah, I stayed." I might have a little more money in my pockets but I wouldn't have tested myself, I wouldn't have been able to say to myself that I had a crack. I am my own harshest critic and I expect the most out of myself and if I don't succeed, I've only got myself to blame. It's a harsh world out there, bro.'

Williams would get an early taste of the harsh treatment he would receive from some sections of the New Zealand media when it emerged that his debut for Canterbury in the ITM Cup would be delayed because of keyhole surgery to tidy up some slight cartilage damage. The procedure was performed the day after Williams knocked out Ryan Hogan in the so-called professional boxing bout in Brisbane. The problem for some was this: if Williams was hell-bent on winning an All Blacks jersey by the end of 2010, why wouldn't he have cancelled the Hogan fight, had the surgery earlier, and been available for Canterbury sooner?

The fact that the Canterbury and New Zealand unions were happy with the arrangement was the first sign that Williams was a special case. 'We knew exactly when it was going to take place and we're just really pleased that it was successful. It's now out of the way and he's going to join us and get on with things,' Canterbury's CEO Hamish Riach said. 'There's no drama or negative angle to this, at all. It was just never an issue. We knew he had his boxing bout, we knew he had this minor keyhole surgery to follow that and then we knew he was going to come [to Christchurch].'

Another criticism came from journalists and punters who were determined to still cast Williams as a mercenary. They argued that the All Blacks jersey — if he earned one — would be a jersey of convenience.

A means to an end for Williams as he chased World Cup glory before leaving New Zealand on the first flight out after the final. That argument was hard to argue against when Sorensen said a successful stint in New Zealand would increase his worth: '[The NZRU] think that Sonny Bill being an All Black ... when he goes back on the market in 2012, he's even more valuable.'

The controversy, though, was all but forgotten when Williams finally played his first game of rugby in his homeland. It wouldn't be for Canterbury, though. It would instead be for Belfast — Smith's old club, which the All Blacks backs coach had recommended Williams align himself with. The club game against Lincoln University at Sheldon Park would be his first game of football in Christchurch since he turned out for Mt Albert Grammar league side against Aranui High 10 years previously.

'It's going to be mind-blowing,' Belfast club manager Norma Eivers told *The Press*. 'The phone hasn't stopped ringing. A lot of people are looking forward to it.' Asked what sort of crowds the club normally attracted, Eivers said: 'Usually ... oh, maybe 100 on a good day.' She said the attendance for the Lincoln game would be 'heaps and heaps. We're in the bottom four, but I'm sure we will go well with Sonny playing. It's going to be a huge treat for all the kids. He came to our game last week and posed for a lot of photos and signed autographs.'

Williams's club coach Don Fisher was still in disbelief that Williams had chosen to play for the unfashionable Belfast club. 'He loves the underdog,' Fisher said. 'You've got to be realistic and honest about it and say Belfast wouldn't be the most appealing club if you were someone of high profile and wanting to go ahead in the game. But the one thing they are out there is genuine people. They're down-to-earth and grassroots and he just feels comfortable in that environment. I've never experienced this type of interest and hype during my time in rugby. We're expecting a lot of people and I think most of them will just be genuinely interested to

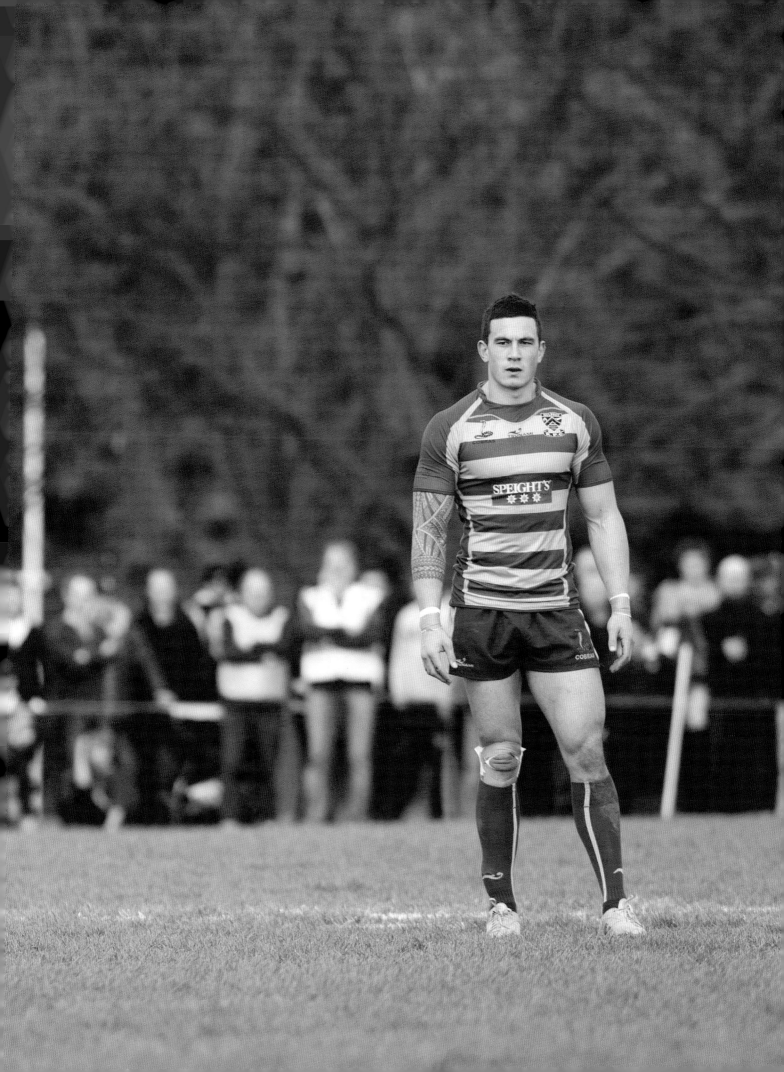

see how he handles the game.'

Such was the interest in the game that the *Sydney Morning Herald*'s Greg Growden — in Christchurch for the Bledisloe Cup test between the All Blacks and the Wallabies — was dispatched to Sheldon Park to report on Williams. This is his match report:

'Sonny Bill Williams went on a New Zealand rugby charm offensive yesterday, luring 4000 spectators to a suburban ground, scoring the try to set up a club victory and giving his backing to the All Blacks winning the Bledisloe Cup stoush. Normally, a Belfast Cobras club match at Sheldon Park on the outskirts of Christchurch lures a few hundred. But the attraction of Sonny Bill's first match in New Zealand, officially starting his campaign to become an All Black, brought them in droves.

'Everyone was there to see Sonny Bill. That was obvious when, after 50 minutes, he was replaced. As he headed to the sideline with a tightening hamstring, almost half the crowd immediately fled. It wasn't quite like when Don Bradman used to get out for a duck, prompting capacity crowds to leave en masse, but Sonny boy certainly enchanted Canterbury. His involvement in the lowly Belfast game against Lincoln University was front-page news yesterday in Christchurch, relegating the Bledisloe Cup to the sports pages. He did enough to please the punters. He made several tackles, threw a few of his characteristic back-hand flick passes, and gave Belfast the lead when he toed through a loose ball and regathered. Minutes later, he was off the field and that was it. Belfast went on to win 22–7.'

Williams relished the hit-out. 'This is what it's all about ... grassroots footy,' Williams said. 'It's good to know people still like me, especially down here where rugby league is not big. I was a bit tired at halftime, but I wanted to give the people their money's worth so I went back out there for another run. It was a good day, I really enjoyed it. It's good to know people know me down here, and are supporting me. That means a lot. And it was great that Belfast got a win at the Snake Pit.'

Williams received an injection of artificial cartilage to his knee two days after his Sheldon Park appearance, a treatment frequently used by footballers with suspect knees. Then the player's critics were given some ammunition when a hamstring injury kept him out of Canterbury's first five games of the season.

Indeed, the *Sunday Star-Times* went as far as to write an article explaining that officials from both Canterbury and the NZRU were 'adamant they have not bought a lemon in Sonny Bill Williams and insist he will make a return to full fitness soon despite the former rugby league international's injury woes'.

In Greg Ford's article, both unions played down the injury news. Canterbury said the injection was a routine treatment to augment the keyhole surgery to his knee and the NZRU, through a spokesman, said Williams had passed two medicals before he signed his contract.

Certainly, the All Blacks selectors were unconcerned. Smith said Williams's chances of making the end-of-year tour would depend on the quality of his performances before the team was set to be named. 'It's probably not the number [of games he plays], it's the quality of them,' Smith said. 'He could go on and blow the competition wide open or he could take a while to settle in. That will be the relevant point.'

Ford and others could be forgiven for being a little anxious. The hype around Williams was unprecedented since the days when newspapermen used to hang off every word uttered from the mouths of Jonah Lomu and his manager Phil Kingsley Jones.

And by late August the scribes finally had something relevant to report on when Williams was deemed fit enough to be selected to play for Canterbury Metro against Canterbury Country at AMI Stadium in the curtain-raiser to the Canterbury ITM Cup game against Auckland. He was given 40 minutes and proved he was ready for a call-up to Rob Penney's team. 'I had scans last week and they said [my right hamstring] came up pretty much perfect,' Williams said after the match. 'Obviously, there's a little bit of

'He could go on and blow

the competition wide open

or he could take a while to settle in.'

pain there, but I've just got to push through it and it's good mentally to know that I can push through the pain. It was definitely a confidence booster out there and, hopefully, for Penz and Tabs [Canterbury coaches Penney and Tabai Matson], I've shown them enough that I can get out there for Canterbury.'

Williams showed a wide range of skills against Country. He threw a number of long accurate passes, scored two tries and looked at ease when he popped into first-receiver half a dozen times. 'That's one thing I really aim to improve on,' Williams said of his skill execution. 'I was happy with it. Obviously, there's always room to improve and I've just got to keep doing what I'm doing and practising the basics so I can fit into the side. It was good being out there and just being able to direct the traffic. That's what I need to show, because in the position I'm aiming to play you need to give good [communication] and give good solutions.'

Another very evident quality on display from Williams was his size. At 191 cm and 110 kg he was clearly significantly bigger than his key rivals for the All Blacks No. 12 jersey, as well as his Wallaby and Springbok Tri-Nations opposites and European counterparts. Indeed, if Williams was good enough to be selected for the All Blacks in their October test against Australia in Hong Kong, and the Wallabies retained Matt Giteau in the No. 12 position, Williams would weigh in a whopping 25 kg heavier than his Aussie rival. He is also 13 cm taller than Giteau. Williams's key rivals for the All Blacks' inside centre position would fare only marginally better than Giteau. Benson Stanley, who made his debut in the role against Ireland last year, and Ma'a Nonu both give away 6 kg to Williams and are much shorter. McAlister would fare even worse, coming in 15 kg lighter than Williams and 11 cm shorter.

Before anyone could get carried away (again), though, SBW reminded the New Zealand public of the circus element that has followed him throughout his career. He was dobbed in when he went skiing

with friends from France while he was on Canterbury's injured list. 'Look, what is done can't be undone,' he would say later. 'My friends were skiing and I got a little carried away and thought I'd give it a go, too. But that's in the past. Now that I'm back on the field I just want to concentrate on rugby.'

McCaw brought a hint of reality to the never-ending hype when he said that just because Williams had made the commitment to play in New Zealand that was no guarantee he would wear the All Blacks jersey. 'He is not going to be picked just because he has decided to come and play rugby,' the influential All Blacks captain said. 'He is going to have to play good enough to prove himself. Some of the guys he will be competing with are pretty good players. He is a hell of an athlete. He is a big man with a lot to offer. It's whether he can fit into how the teams play or not. I could imagine if we help him as much as possible — firstly, in the Canterbury set-up and then the Crusaders — he can be a real handful. A couple of guys who played him in Toulon say he is a real threat every time he gets the ball. I'm intrigued to see how he goes.'

Williams would get on the track for Canterbury against Bay of Plenty when he came off the bench at AMI Stadium for Ryan Crotty after 18 minutes and immediately impressed with his passing ability and defensive strength. He showed several good touches — intercepting a pass on defence and setting up an attacking move which Nasi Manu ended with a try in the 28–9 win.

Those attacking qualities were on show in Whangarei a week later when Williams was given his first start for his new province in the No. 12 jersey. His combination with outside centre Robbie Fruean had sparked much interest the previous weekend and after Canterbury's 27–23 victory it was at fever pitch. Williams had a hand in all of the side's three first-half tries — the first a brilliant offload to Fruean. It was a good 'pop' from SBW, but it was nothing compared with the miracle ball he produced for Luke Romano's try, while Isaac

Sonny Bill Williams — All Black, 2010. An impressive ITM Cup campaign meant he was always going to picked for the All Blacks' end-of-year tour to Ireland and Britain.

Ross was the other beneficiary of a Williams pass for his pre-break try.

Williams wasn't just impressing his new teammates and coaching staff. After the game at Okara Park he was mobbed by excited youngsters, in a throwback to the days of the great North Auckland teams stacked with names like Johnny Smith, Peter Jones, Sid Going, Joe Morgan and Rupeni Caucaunibuca.

It was heady stuff for Williams, but provincial rugby has a habit of producing nasty surprises and for the Red 'n Blacks it came at Yarrow Stadium the following week. Taranaki were celebrating their 125th anniversary and celebrate they did. They served up

Canterbury's first loss of the season (31–20) and despite some strong and decisive running against the 'Naki — which was rewarded with his first try in New Zealand via a pass from Andy Ellis — the second-five with a growing reputation found himself benched the following weekend when Wellington visited Christchurch.

Crotty — the incumbent second five-eighth before Williams's arrival in Canterbury — was fit again and Penney slipped him back into the starting XV. Williams wasn't thrilled. And neither were the 30,000-plus spectators who took advantage of the free entry granted for the game as the Canterbury Rugby Football

Union, AMI Insurance, Tui, Vbase and Ticket Direct moved to do something for their public who had lived through the province's 7.1-magnitude earthquake three weeks earlier. Their dissatisfaction with Williams's benching was made perfectly clear by the cheer which engulfed AMI Stadium when he ran out with the team at the start of the second half. At the time Canterbury trailed Wellington by 20–13. By the end of the game Williams had scored the game-winning try after stepping inside Lima Sopoaga, palming off one-time All Blacks prop John Schwalger and going through Charlie Ngatai. A Colin Slade penalty put the seal on the famous 37–30 triumph. Interestingly, to further aid the victims of the earthquake, each jersey worn by the Canterbury players was auctioned off to raise money. The jersey which received the highest bid ($5050) was jersey No. 22 — SBW's.

Williams's combination with Fruean had many pundits predicting both men would make the All Blacks tour. 'He's a great player,' Williams said of Fruean. 'You've just got to look at him and the way he plays to know that. I try to give him the ball early and then run off him. It's awesome being in this environment because there's not just Robbie, there is Stephen Brett and there are players with X-factor all over the place. I'm just happy to be among it here.'

SBW was among it a few days later at Carisbrook — where he would be mobbed by excited fans again — when he was the pick of the bunch for Canterbury in their straightforward 35–20 win against Otago. Ironically, he was in the team at centre — with Fruean relegated to the bench. He set up a try for Tu Umaga-Marshall before, in the second half, he received a pass from Slade, stepped inside the defence and showed great speed and footwork to make it the 50 metres to the tryline.

Williams was back in the No. 12 jersey for the team's next outing at Rugby Park. Rugby Southland chief executive Roger Clark confirmed that the usual complement of security personnel would be employed for the shield match, which included six

people patrolling the infield. He said security would be specifically instructed to watch out for the players on the field immediately after the game. 'There was a bit of a shemozzle at Carisbrook last weekend when other players had to protect [Williams] rather than the security doing it. It's all right to let the fans run onto the field, but it's no good if it puts the players under any sort of threat. They weren't little kids, they were big kids who were all over him and for any of the players we have to make sure we protect their safety.'

By the end of the encounter Canterbury were back atop the ITM Cup points table, had secured a home semifinal and had won back the Ranfurly Shield from the side that had taken it from them in 2009. The historic encounter was dominated by the battle between the two packs, and while Williams didn't have too many opportunities on attack he impressed with his discipline and work ethic on defence.

It was a significant day for Williams because it is unlikely he will ever challenge for the Shield again as he isn't expected to be involved in New Zealand rugby after the 2011 World Cup — a year when All Blacks won't be required for ITM Cup duty. Still, after only six games, he was, and forever will be, a part of Canterbury's proud Ranfurly Shield history. It's a history which dates back to the 1927 season when they won and lost it within two games and takes in 12 other eras including 1931–34 (with 15 successful defences), 1935 (four), 1950 (zero), 1953–56 (23), 1969–71 (nine), 1972–73 (two), 1982–85 (25), 1994–95 (nine), 2000–03 (23), 2004–06 (14), 2007 (one) and 2009 (seven).

The win only added to the growing legend of 'Sonny Bill Williams' in the Mainland and around the country. He was in huge demand from corporations — he had just done a deal with Rebel Sport for a series of commercials. New Zealand Tourism was also showing an interest to enlist SBW in an advertising campaign, and a number of athletic brands had approached him to do clothing and shoe deals. He was also being courted heavily by media outlets desperate to have

SHIELD FEVER

Canterbury won the Ranfurly Shield for the fourteenth time when they defeated Southland at Rugby Park on 9 October 2010. It was Sonny Bill Williams's first piece of silverware in New Zealand rugby.

TEAMS

Canterbury: Sean Maitland, Tu Umaga-Marshall, Robbie Fruean, *Sonny Bill Williams*, Telusa Veainu, Colin Slade, Andy Ellis (captain), Nasi Manu, Matt Todd, Sam Whitelock, Isaac Ross, Luke Romano, Peter Borlase, Corey Flynn, Wyatt Crockett. *Reserves*: Steve Fualau, Andrew Olorenshaw, Ash Parker, Brendon O'Connor, Willi Heinz, Stephen Brett, Ryan Crotty.

Southland: Glen Horton, Mark Wells, Matt Saunders, James Wilson, Tony Koonwaiyou, Robbie Robinson, Jimmy Cowan, Kane Thompson, Tim Boys, John Hardie, Joe Tuineau, Josh Bekhuis, Chris King, Jason Rutledge, Jamie Mackintosh (captain). *Reserves*: David Hall, Nick Barrett, Alex Ryan, Hua Tamariki, Scott Cowan, Seminar Manu, Pehi Te Whare.

SCORERS

Southland 16 (K. Thompson try; R. Robinson con, 2 pens; J. Wilson pen).
Canterbury 26 (T. Veainu, C. Slade tries; C. Slade 2 cons, 4 pens).
Halftime: Canterbury, 16–13.

PREVIOUS PAGES: Sonny Bill Williams in action for Canterbury against Bay of Plenty, Counties Manukau, and Southland (right).

him on their TV screens and in their papers. His brand was already so powerful that the old 'don't hate him because he's beautiful' line — made famous in New Zealand by a *NZ Rugby World* cover of All Black Doug Howlett's face being licked by two models in 2001 — was evoked by the *New Zealand Herald* staffer Michael Guerin in their first edition following the victory in Southland.

'You can be forgiven for not liking him,' Guerin wrote. 'I don't want to like him, not somebody this unfairly talented. With his super-charmed life, those looks, the insane ability, the international media profile. All style and magazine shoots and adoring young fans. And now the monster that is Canterbury rugby has beat up its brave little Southland cousins, he has the Ranfurly Shield to play with as well. Hardly seems fair when the snow-shovelling, real men of the South lose their most treasured possession to guys like him from Canterbury. Yes, it would be easy not to like him. A man so outrageously blessed he was destined to wear the black jersey from the time he was old enough to drive. A man so special he can skive off to go play for some Frog team nobody had ever heard of, leaving his mates at Canterbury to fend for themselves. And then he returns to New Zealand to a guaranteed All Black jersey. And he has the guile to do all this while enjoying his life. Being happy, learning languages. The modelling, the topless photo shoots. It is easy to dislike a man like this. A man who plays a sport that is supposed to take a heavy physical toll, but still looks like an Adonis.

'It is easy to not like this man, knowing your girlfriend might occasionally catch a glance of him on TV or a billboard and then consider buying you the Abmaster 2000. What makes it worse is knowing that, if you played golf with him, he's the sort of guy who would downplay his exploits, be polite and funny. Then outdrive you by 50 metres. He's the sort of guy whose friends call him by his initials. I mean really, what sort of rugby player is that? You wouldn't have heard Colin Meads or Wayne Shelford getting called by some silly nickname, would you? This is rugby, not boxing, after all. And yet he's always so self-effacing on television, with that constant smile, boy-next-door manners and the trendy clothes. Yes, it is easy to dislike a man like this.

'And why Canterbury? Why is he playing for the red-and-blacks, who have so much talent in his position alone, when he could have come to Auckland? We wanted him, but instead he plays for the one team that could win without him. And we all know he is far more Auckland than Canterbury. You know what makes this envy worse. He will soon be jetting off to the northern hemisphere with the All Blacks, where he will destroy his opponents and further boost his asking price for his post World Cup career. And when he gets there, he will have that other glamour boy outside him. That one called Sonny Bill Williams.

'Yes, it would be easy not to like a man like Dan Carter. A man who has done all those things you just read and yet is just still on his way to rugby sainthood. But of course nobody dislikes Carter. Because he's a great guy. Because he plays his rugby like a violent ballet, has bled for his country and because you know the next year of his life is dedicated to winning us the World Cup. Which makes you wonder why some people — rugby traditionalists they call themselves — dislike Sonny Bill Williams. And want to see him fail so they can say "we told you so".

'When you think about it, are DC and SWB really that different? Sure, one is already an All Black legend but the other one hasn't had that chance yet. Yet. And considering how SBW has conducted himself on and off the field since coming home, what's not to like? Unless of course you come from Southland, because he just stole your shield. ...'

Just as significant for Williams as the Ranfurly Shield win was his next game for Canterbury. The visitors to Christchurch were Counties Manukau and the man marshalling their backline for their Shield challenge was none other than Tana Umaga. Before the game Williams's Toulon mentor said his star pupil had gone a long way towards achieving his All Black goal. 'I think he will make the All Blacks,' Umaga said. 'He is playing great rugby and everyone is singing his praises as I knew they would.'

In the game it was very much a case of the master passing the baton on to the apprentice as SBW fended off Umaga to score a try and help secure the 39–21 win. It was Williams's fourth try in seven games and overall the best of any of his performances. 'When I first came here, I think people thought I was just going to try to smash blokes,' said Williams after the contest. 'The biggest thing I'm trying to overcome is getting out of the mindset of trying to smash blokes.'

The following day it was time for Henry, Hansen and Smith to name their All Blacks touring team. All the hype leading up to and following his signing with the NZRU had come down to an announcement at Eden Park on a Sunday in October.

FOR the modern-day rugby centre there are two endorsements you covet — that of Frank Bunce and that of Tana Umaga.

Bunce, of course, followed in the footsteps of men like Bruce Robertson and Smokin' Joe Stanley as he set a new standard for the All Blacks' No. 13 jersey in 69 games for the team between 1992 and 1997. Brutal on defence with an ability to be elusive on attack (read: two of the great All Blacks midfield tries against the Springboks at Ellis Park in Johannesburg in 1997), Bunce was anointed the Prince of Centres — a crown he wore with a comfortable ease.

Umaga, on the other hand, can't lay claim to being one of the great centres of All Blacks rugby. He was a very good All Black but his greatness was tied to his leadership abilities. And, it could be argued, in the captaincy stakes he can lay claim to being in the top six of all time behind men like Wayne Shelford, Wilson Whineray, Sean Fitzpatrick, Richie McCaw and Graham Mourie. His finest moments in black came in 2005 when he led the All Blacks to one of its greatest years as he and his charges held on to the Bledisloe Cup, won the Tri-Nations, black-washed the British and Irish Lions and claimed New Zealand's second Grand Slam with end-of-year wins in England, Scotland, Ireland and Wales.

By the time Graham Henry was ready to name his squad for the 2010 side's attempt at a Grand Slam of their own, Sonny Bill Williams had won praise from both.

Umaga — Williams's original coach at Toulon — had been thrilled with Williams's progress over his seven appearances for Canterbury. 'His name will definitely be read out,' Umaga said on the eve of Henry's announcement. 'I think he's playing great rugby and I'm sure everyone else has seen what he can offer. He was a bit nervous when he first came over and he did have his critics but he's actually shown that he does have some amazing ability. He went to Canterbury to be in the right environment to grow, and I believe he's done that. When he gets into the All Blacks environment I think he'll see how much more he can improve. We'll see whether he can foot it at the international level, but I don't see him having any problems. With the group he's with I think he'll flourish. He's doing well at Canterbury and he'll continue to do well after he gets named and I wish him all the best for that.'

Bunce, too, was convinced Williams could be a hit in the test arena. He told RadioLIVE's Martin Devlin that SBW had the potential to help deliver a World Cup to New Zealand. 'He has the X-factor — no doubt about that,' he told *Devlin on Sport*. 'Everyone knew before he played a game for Canterbury that he was big and strong. What we didn't know was that he had a great passing game and one of the best offloads in either rugby or league. The thought of him being unleashed for the All Blacks with someone like Richie McCaw running off him is pretty exciting. He will be named in the All Blacks touring team. And I have to say that I can't wait to see how he goes at the test level.'

PUSHING THE BOUNDARIES

IT WAS the text messages that gave it away. Sonny Bill Williams's flight from Christchurch to Auckland had been delayed, so he didn't arrive in the City of Sails until after the NZRU's chairman Mike Eagle had read out Graham Henry's 30-strong touring party. 'As soon as I turned my phone on about 20 messages popped up. The first one was from the old lady and she was pretty happy.'

Williams was beaming as he was surrounded by journalists from both sides of the Tasman. 'I think when I first went to rugby I had a lot of self-doubts, thinking I don't know if I can make it or not, and it's all turned out really good. I'm just trying to soak it up at the moment. The big thing for me coming back here was the amount of support I've got from the public. Not just in Canterbury, but going to places like Whangarei and Southland and little kids coming up to me knowing my name. That's really helped my self-confidence and as a person to grow.'

Williams was in no doubt that the smartest decision he made in his transition from Toulon was picking Canterbury as his base. 'I'm happy with picking Canterbury to go to. And I think it has paid dividends to get into that system straight away. I've really taken to the boys and hopefully they've taken to me, too. I've come on leaps and bounds. I made it a point when I came back here that I really wanted to work on the distribution part of my game because when you watch players like Ma'a Nonu, who's the best midfielder in New Zealand, you see that he can break a tackle, he can put players into gaps and that's what I wanted to add to my game. My understanding of the game has got a lot better, I believe. I feel like a rugby player now, rather than a league player playing rugby union — especially at Canterbury. I understand the system, I understand where the ball needs to go and what I am really enjoying at the moment is being able to distribute as well. I am never going to be a typical No. 12, but if the ball needs to go wide I can put it wide; if I am going to have a crack I will have a crack. I just try to do the basics real well and if I can continue to do that then anything is possible.

Sonny Bill Williams fulfilled a lifelong dream in November 2010 when he made his debut for the All Blacks against England at Twickenham.

'Making this squad is the first step, but I still have to prove myself. The ITM Cup is not international level so I still have a lot to prove. But I pride myself in having a crack, and that is what I am going to be doing. I just want to get in the system and learn as much as I can. I have got to be a sponge and learn off all the boys. All the way I have tried to learn off as many people as I can, I have never been close-minded or arrogant, and that has got me further than I ever expected at this stage. So, I've still got a lot to learn and this is only the first phase, but you won't be wiping the smile off my face tonight.

'It is an awesome feeling. This is the biggest thing that has happened in my sporting career. My uncle rang and said, "I am proud of your achievements. Now I can go around saying my nephew is an All Black." I still haven't run out in the black jersey, but it is a humbling feeling just knowing that I am in the squad. It is a desire I probably had as a youngster before I started playing league. I remember watching the 1995 World Cup and wanting to be an All Black, but it didn't feel like it was in my blood to play rugby. That is why I am so thankful to Tana Umaga because I

TOUR OF DUTY

The All Blacks squad for the 2010 tour of Hong Kong, England, Scotland, Ireland and Wales included only one debutant — Sonny Bill Williams.

Forwards: John Afoa, Anthony Boric, Daniel Braid, Tom Donnelly, Hikawera Elliot, Ben Franks, Owen Franks, Andrew Hore, Jerome Kaino, Richie McCaw (captain), Keven Mealamu, Liam Messam, Kieran Read, Brad Thorn, Samuel Whitelock, Tony Woodcock.
Backs: Andy Ellis, Daniel Carter, Jimmy Cowan, Stephen Donald, Hosea Gear, Cory Jane, Alby Mathewson, Mils Muliaina, Ma'a Nonu, Josevata Rokocoko, Sitiveni Sivivatu, Conrad Smith, Isaia Toeava, *Sonny Bill Williams*.

wasn't thinking anything about rugby, all I was thinking about was getting out of the situation I was in, and then all of a sudden I got a call from him. It all just went from there. Once I went to rugby I had to reassess my goals and things like that, and I wanted to reach the pinnacle of playing rugby for a Kiwi.'

Williams also praised fellow All Blacks league convert Brad Thorn and revealed that the former Broncos star's successful transition to the All Blacks ranks was a factor in his decision to join the Crusaders. 'He is a real good man, old Thorny,' Williams told the *Sydney Morning Herald*. 'All of the boys love him. I met him back in league when I played against him, but I didn't really know him. But before I came down to Christchurch he told all of the young boys, "You make sure you look after Sonny," and he made sure I felt at home. One of the reasons I came to Canterbury was seeing the way he has done it. I have been privileged to play alongside Tana Umaga and some great players at Toulon, but Thorny is right up there. He would be one of the best locks in the game at the moment.'

The turning point in Williams's career was meeting All Blacks assistant coach Wayne Smith in France in 2009. 'Smithy was over in France seeing Dan Carter [at Perpignan] and he happened to stop by and see Tana and we caught up for a coffee,' Williams said. 'Then Graham Henry and Wayne Smith had the foresight and belief in me that I could probably do something. It's been a tough road and a lot of hard work, but I'm just proud because this is the biggest achievement I've ever had in my sporting career.'

And it hadn't all been plain sailing. The surgery following Williams's bout and the injuries that followed his debut for Belfast had taken their toll. 'That was a difficult time when I first came back here. The toughest

Sonny Bill Williams was helped through his early days as an All Black by another former league star — All Blacks teammate Brad Thorn.

'I have the utmost respect for the guy.

He is a very unselfish rugby player on the

field and he has made a big impression

in the Canterbury province ...'

thing about it was that I thought my knee was sweet and I just thought while I was back in Brisbane, my doctor is up there so I'd get everything checked out before I went to New Zealand. They X-rayed my arm that I broke back in 2005, X-rayed my leg that I broke the year before and just had all these other tests. Everything was sweet except for the MRI on my knee. I couldn't even feel it and it wasn't bothering me, but the doc just said if I leave it there was a chance it could get a lot worse. That was disappointing finding out just a week before I went over to New Zealand because I wanted to get out there and show my teammates that I can play, and that I am worth all of the fuss.'

While Sonny Bill Williams, All Black, was holding court with the press in one corner of the conference room at Eden Park, the All Blacks coach was talking to SkyTV and was happily defending the All Blacks' newcomer against those who were still inclined to put a '$' before the 'BW' when referring to rugby's latest superstar. 'He only got probably about 25 per cent of what he could have got in Europe [when he signed with the NZRU], so I think it is the complete opposite of a mercenary,' Henry said. 'I have the utmost respect for the guy. He is a very unselfish rugby player on the field and he has made a big impression in the Canterbury province ... "mercenary" would be the last thing that I would say about him.'

Williams's elevation to the All Blacks was big news in Australia. And one Australian, more than any other it seems, was gutted. Not because of any preference for rugby league. No. Eddie Jones was gutted for the Wallabies because he couldn't understand why they hadn't entered the race to sign him earlier in the year. 'The All Blacks have a whole new attacking weapon on their hands,' the former Wallabies coach told the *Sydney Morning Herald*. 'When most players go into a tackle, on three occasions out of 10 they will get an offload away. When Sonny hits the line, it's seven out of 10. That will give the All Blacks the ability to bust up a defence and will allow them to attack in a whole new way. There is no better player in world rugby at getting

Eddie Jones, the former Wallabies coach, still can't understand why the ARU didn't pursue Sonny Bill Williams with the same vigour as their New Zealand counterparts.

an offload away than Sonny Bill.'

As the tour loomed the focus on Williams only intensified. The first of the team's five tests was the fourth Bledisloe Cup test which was to be played in Hong Kong. With the All Blacks already 3–0 ahead in the series there was nothing — other than pride and momentum — riding on the meeting between the New Zealand and Australian sides. In that sense it seemed like the perfect opportunity to introduce Williams to test football.

Without doubt, the Wallabies expected him to play. Their gifted first-five, the Tokoroa-born Quade Cooper, had labelled the possibility of coming up against his mate SBW as 'scary' as he warned teammates not to take the league convert lightly. 'When I found out Sonny Bill was picked in that All Blacks squad I sent him a text straightaway to say congratulations — he's a top bloke and he's been playing good footy,' Cooper told the *Sun-Herald*. 'I'm where I'm at now because I was lucky enough to go on the spring tour last year, and I think Sonny will benefit just as much. Coming into a World Cup, you want to play against the best nations — the Wallabies, the Springboks and then a spring tour of the power nations. It's going to be great for him, and I know he'll really enjoy it and turn into an even better player than what he is now. It's going to be scary. And him running off Dan Carter, that's not something I like thinking about. But for him, being part of that set-up, for his personal development it's going to work wonders for Sonny. It's scary enough thinking about tackling him in a week's time, but it's going to be a very scary prospect to see where he is at in 12 months.'

Cooper and Williams were cut from the same cloth when it came to their rugby philosophy. 'Rugby is something that we love doing and we want entertainment factor for the fans. And if you can bring that entertainment factor to your game with players like Sonny Bill, it's going to be pretty exciting for the fans. I think he's making the transition well, and from what he's told me, he's starting to really enjoy it now.'

Even before the All Blacks left for Asia the debate raged as to whether he should start the game on the bench or in the starting XV. Williams, though, certainly wasn't caught up in the debate. 'Even if I don't get in the team to play, just lining up and training with them day in, day out, learning off some of the best players in the world, I would be happy just with that,' he told Fairfax. 'If I don't get a game on tour, I will still be better off from it. There is such a lot of talent out there that I have to prove myself on this tour. If they give me a shot, I've really got to learn so that when I come back, God willing I don't get injured, and I can roll off this into a good Super 15 and stay in the frame. Don't get me wrong, it's about trying to play for the All Blacks and achieve a childhood dream to try to get a foot in the door before the World Cup ... but it is not just all about that. For me, pride plays a lot in my decisions. If I didn't care about that stuff, I could have gone back to France on real good money and fly under the radar and hide.

'Coming back was about proving myself. Because I had proven myself in rugby league. Ask any player when you talk about what it means, to a lot of them it is family and things like that. That's big for me, but my pride is [important], too, and when all I hear is that "he's a shit rugby player", you block it out to some extent but it also hurts your pride a bit. It becomes: "I want to show you, and sod it, I will go back there and do it."

'To be honest, when I first went to Toulon I didn't really have that burning desire because it was all foreign to me. But now I love the game. The same way I used to love playing league I now love playing rugby. If I stop playing rugby for Crusaders or Toulon or whoever today, I would go down and sign up just to play in a local comp. And I would be signing up to play rugby union because I like it, especially the way they play it in New Zealand.'

Williams, however, would have to wait to experience how the All Blacks played as he was, surprisingly, left out of the team to play in Hong Kong. Henry said he was reluctant to toss him into the 'deep end' of test rugby. Instead Nonu and Conrad Smith were named in the centres with Isaia Toeava covering off the bench. Henry said, 'We think he needs a bit of time to get

Before Sonny Bill Williams got to make his debut for the All Blacks he was forced to sit in the stands and watch his new teammates suffer their only defeat of 2010 — against the Wallabies in Hong Kong.

ALL BLACKS v Australia at Hong Kong Stadium, Hong Kong, on 30 October 2010.
All Blacks: **Mils Muliaina, Cory Jane, Conrad Smith, Ma'a Nonu, Josevata Rokocoko, Daniel Carter, Jimmy Cowan, Kieran Read, Richie McCaw (captain), Jerome Kaino, Tom Donnelly, Brad Thorn, Owen Franks, Keven Mealamu, Tony Woodcock.**
Reserves: **Hikawera Elliot, John Afoa, Samuel Whitelock, Daniel Braid, Alby Mathewson, Stephen Donald, Isaia Toeava.**

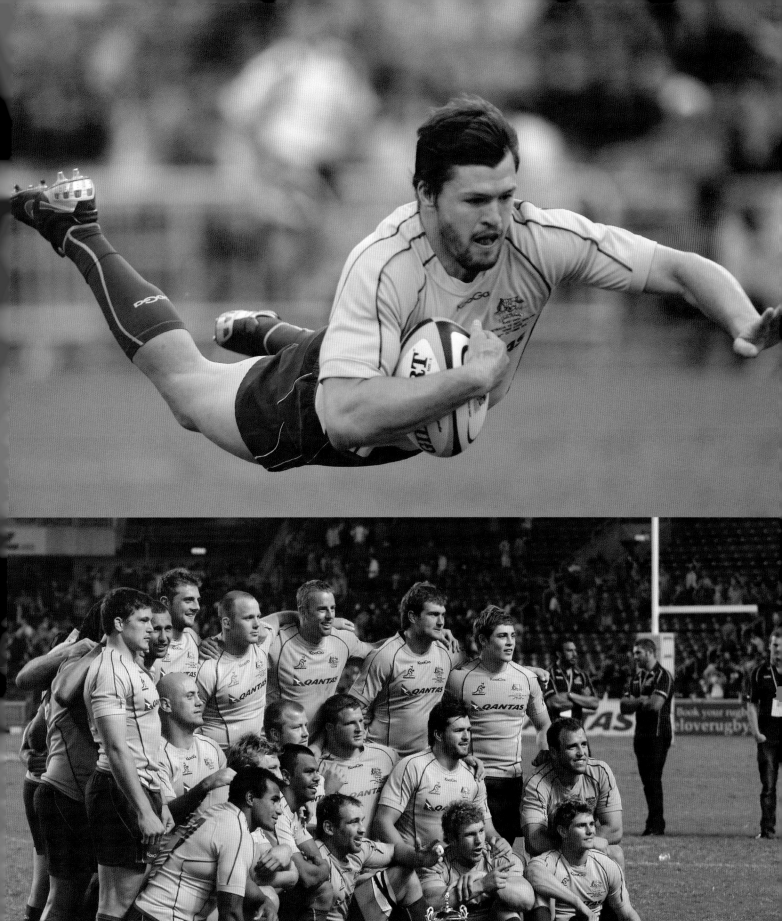

accustomed to what we are trying to do out there and I think he needs clarity of what this All Blacks team are trying to do. It would have been a big ask to throw him out there in a big test match like this without having time to get his feet under the table. It takes a wee bit of a while to get clarity on what the team is trying to do. You need to understand the game plan, the team culture and what we are trying to do out there. And that is natural. It is just going to take time.'

As it was, it wasn't a bad test to sit out. The All Blacks chose this occasion to put in their least productive performance of the year as they allowed the Wallabies to come from behind to snatch a famous 26–24 win with the last kick of the match.

The All Blacks' 10-game winning streak against Robbie Deans' side was over. Momentum was lost. The fragile New Zealand rugby public were all of a sudden worried about the team's World Cup prospects as the airwaves were suddenly full of questions like: *Can the All Blacks go up a gear or have they already peaked? Are Brad Thorn, Keven Mealamu and Mils Muliaina too old? Will we ever have back-ups for Dan Carter and Richie McCaw?*

Rugby needed a distraction. Quickly. And a week later in London, a former Canterbury-Bankstown Bulldog would provide it.

FINALLY. The moment had come. Sonny Bill Williams would, Graham Henry had determined, pull on the famous All Blacks jersey for the first time. The city was London and the opposition was England. And, appropriately, the game would be played at Twickenham — one of the biggest and grandest stages of any in rugby.

It was the culmination of a boyhood dream. And it was much more than that. It was, without a doubt, vindication for Khoder Nasser and Anthony Mundine — Williams's much vilified cohorts in his exit from the Bulldogs two years earlier.

Their advice, the critics argued, had ruined Williams. They said his head had been turned by the greed of the boxing promoter and his upstart superstar.

But, respectfully, how bad was the advice to get out of the Canterbury-Bankstown deal? Within two years Williams had made close to NZ$3 million and was about to wear the All Blacks jersey in a test match for the first time.

Bad advice?

Hardly.

THE one-time man-child was now something akin to a man-mountain. He stood at 1.91 m and tipped the scales at 108 kg. A lean, mean, fighting machine if ever there was one. But Sonny Bill Williams was, for a week at least, reduced to a reincarnation of a schoolboy in the week leading up to his first test for the All Blacks.

The solitary new cap on the All Blacks' Grand Slam tour had plenty of 'learnings' to endure as he tried to get up to speed with the All Blacks game plan. 'It's pretty intense,' Williams said. 'I've never experienced anything like this before. The biggest difference to when I played at the top level in league is here you notice how different the games are. League's a pretty simple game. In rugby there is a whole lot of set-pieces, scrums, backs moves and such to cover. It's been a big learning curve. I just try to be like a sponge. It's just like school. I go home, get that notepad out and jot things down. Last week [in Hong Kong] was pretty tough; it was like a teething process. At the moment I'm feeling pretty confident with all the moves and what we're trying to achieve on the field.'

Jonny Wilkinson — the great England first-five — was a teammate of Williams's for a year in Toulon and he sought out the former league player to give him some encouragement ahead of his test debut. 'You can't get complacent' was the message Wilkinson

All Blacks coach Graham Henry liked what he saw in the build-up to the Twickenham test, and found room for Sonny Bill Williams in the All Blacks' backline.

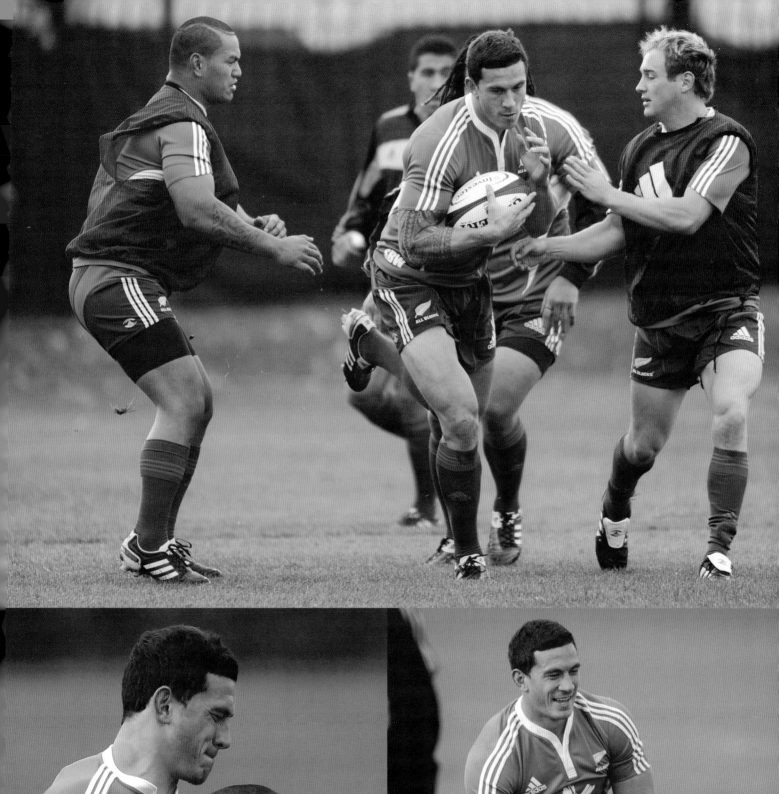

'... the All Blacks were definitely the pinnacle for

any person playing rugby. The All Blacks jersey

was the one I wanted to get.'

gave, as told by Williams. 'As soon as you start thinking you're in that team or in the 30-man squad, that you're going to get picked, that's when you tend to let your foot off the pedal.'

It was Wilkinson's arrival at Toulon that coincided with an upturn in fortunes for Williams. Playing outside the 2003 World Cup winning hero and listening to him talk about what it meant to him to play for his country served two purposes: it helped Williams's understanding of rugby and cemented his desire to wear the black jersey.

'When I first went to Toulon I was injured a lot so I didn't know if I could cut it. The second year, stringing 20 games together, that gave me a lot of confidence,' Williams said. 'That's the reason I wanted to go back [to New Zealand] and have a crack, to prove to people, and myself, that I could play. I was fortunate to play alongside some greats — Jonny, Tana Umaga, (Juan) Fernandez Lobbe, Felipe Contepomi, Joe van Niekerk. Playing around those guys really helped because I knew they had reached the top. Being able to play alongside those guys really helped my confidence. I had the feeling I could mix it with the best, but for me the best players were still playing back home in New Zealand.

'When I left [the Bulldogs] I didn't care where I was going. It was just about getting out of the situation I was in. Fortunately, Tana Umaga had the foresight that I could play rugby. Playing over there, I had to change my goals and the All Blacks were definitely the pinnacle for any person playing rugby. The All Blacks jersey was the one I wanted to get.'

Despite most of his rugby in the ITM Cup coming at second five-eight, Graham Henry picked Williams at centre for his debut test. He would play outside Ma'a Nonu against England. And that was significant because Nonu — the incumbent No. 12 in the team — had been more than generous in helping out the All Blacks' newbie at every turn. 'Ma'a has really taken me under his wing on the finer points of what we're trying to achieve as All Blacks,' Williams said. 'From the outside coming in I was probably a bit anxious to

see what the boys were like. Everyone's been great. You ask a question, you get 10 answers ...'

Williams was one of four changes from the side beaten by Australia in Hong Kong, allowing him to become the first Kiwis international to represent the All Blacks — in that order — since Karl Ifwersen played the third test against the Springboks in 1921, a year after ending his 10-test league career. Hurricanes wing Hosea Gear replaced the injured Cory Jane, while Blues halfback Alby Mathewson came in for Jimmy Cowan, who had failed to make the 22 for the game at Twickenham. The other change saw second-rower Sam Whitelock replace Tom Donnelly in the pack, where he would partner another former rugby league player, Brad Thorn.

'There is a resolve in the team to put in an improved performance this weekend and the team has worked hard on that this week,' All Blacks coach Graham Henry said. And Steve Hansen — the team's forward coach — was relishing the chance to see his charges take on an England team which pre-match had boasted about playing tough and uncompromising 'old-fashioned' rugby designed to restrict the All Blacks' open style.

'I think England would be happy to go from set-piece to set-piece to set-piece, so they can take us on in that area and see if they can beat us,' Hansen told reporters in his weekly briefing with the media.

ALL BLACKS v England at Twickenham, London, on 6 November 2010.

All Blacks: Mils Muliaina, Joe Rokocoko, *Sonny Bill Williams*, Ma'a Nonu, Hosea Gear, Dan Carter, Alby Mathewson, Kieran Read, Richie McCaw (captain), Jerome Kaino, Sam Whitelock, Brad Thorn, Owen Franks, Keven Mealamu, Tony Woodcock.

Reserves: Hika Elliot, Ben Franks, Anthony Boric, Liam Messam, Andy Ellis, Stephen Donald and Isaia Toeava.

'We know from experience year after year that when we play England they will be very physical up front and we've got to match that and get on top of it. That is the type of game they want to play and we can't back away from it — but that doesn't stop us from playing our own style of rugby.'

Before the test Henry moved to dismiss the stories doing the rounds comparing Sonny Bill Williams and All Black legend Jonah Lomu, saying the rugby league convert still had much to prove. 'I don't think we should get ahead of ourselves,' Henry said. 'There's a huge gap between domestic rugby and international rugby. I'm sure there are a lot of areas in the game that he will need to sharpen up on to be a great international player. He's a big person, he's obviously very strong, he's got the ability to offload well in a contact situation, so he might add an extra dimension there.'

Hansen, too, urged restraint when SBW's debut was dissected. 'It's going to be a big test for him; this is a different level of rugby to what he's used to. Sometimes it takes a bit of time; I don't think we can be too critical. We've just got to ease him into it. We know he's a great athlete and he's got some special qualities. One of those is his attitude. He's a pretty humble young man; his feet are firmly on the floor.'

Hansen was then asked how, as a former representative centre, he would keep Williams's imposing frame firmly on the ground. 'Aw shit, I never would have been good enough,' he admitted. 'You'd have to take a team approach; he's six foot four, a big explosive athlete. His time in league has given him that ability to be able to keep the ball alive. He's got hands on him like ham sandwiches; he can hang on to the ball in one hand ... I think you're going to need someone high and someone low [when you tackle him].'

The closest Williams had got to an All Blacks test before the tour began had come a year earlier when he was still a Toulon player and was left standing outside Marseille Stadium listening to the team perform the haka. 'We rocked down from Toulon to watch the All Blacks play France. There was Fotu Auelua, Mafi Kefu, Matt Henjak and me, and we were all excited but we couldn't get in because one of the boys had forgotten the tickets. We got there and Fotu pulled an envelope out of his pocket with the tickets, but it was his electricity bill or his water bill or something. We were standing outside the stadium looking around and thinking what we could do, and then we heard

the haka so we just went home. It's funny now, but I was gutted at the time.'

At Twickenham the All Blacks, predictably, were too good for England, winning 26–16. As the scoreline suggests, it was a stuttering performance from the New Zealanders. And, as the pre-match hype had indicated, much of the focus went on one Sonny Bill Williams during and after the test. Despite a solid

Sonny Bill Williams follows Ma'a Nonu out of the Twickenham tunnel as he runs out as an All Black for the first time.
FOLLOWING PAGES: The anthem, haka and action for the All Blacks' newest recruit.

first-up game in black — including one masterclass in the art of the offload when he handed off to Mils Muliaina in space during a movement that led to Gear's try, Williams admonished himself for not being more involved, especially as the pace of the game began to eat into his fitness levels.

'I was disappointed in my own performance and there are a lot of things I can improve on,' he told Fairfax's Richard Knowler. 'But it is just like when I came back and started in New Zealand. Hopefully, it will be like a snowball effect where I get a bit more game time and express myself a lot more. The fitness levels will definitely be a bit better in the next couple of weeks if I get a bit of game time and inject myself a lot more. I just hope to get a bit more game time and improve on that performance. But in the next couple of hours I am just going to sit back and be proud of myself for accomplishing what I said I would do at the start.'

When lining up for the haka, which was drowned out by around 80,000 fans singing 'Swing Low, Sweet Chariot', Williams stood near the back and admitted there had been a surge of emotions as he lined up for the national anthems. 'I was just thinking about the time when this team was so far away. Just being out there it was all sinking in. I didn't want to let my family, you know, the ones dear to me, down — and the people that gave me this opportunity.'

The man responsible for his selection certainly wasn't as harsh on Williams as the 25-year-old had been on himself. 'Sonny will be a better player for the experience,' Henry said. 'He did break the line a couple of times. I don't think he's entirely happy with his game, but that's probably what you expect after your first game in front of 82,000 at Twickenham. I'm pretty happy with what he did.'

Knowler — one of the best analysts of rugby in

Sonny Bill Williams on the burst against England as the All Blacks stormed to a 26–16 win at Twickenham in London.

'I just hope to get a bit more game time and improve on that performance. But in the next couple of hours I am just going to sit back and be proud of myself for accomplishing what I said I would do at the start.'

the New Zealand media — captured the vibe around Williams perfectly with his post-game wrap in the Christchurch's *Press*. 'It was not a flawless effort, and [Williams] knew it. A wild Joe Rokocoko pass would have been taken had Williams bothered to stick two hands in the air instead of one. Instead the ball rolled into touch. He was also beaten in the air by Mike Tindall after he was targeted from a kick-off, appeared uncertain in defence on one occasion, and a grubber kick he executed was largely ineffectual. Yet Williams's worth to this side, before and during the World Cup, could be immense, and one can only wonder how much more he will improve once he has got through next year's Super 15 campaign with the Crusaders.

'Speaking to the media pack inside Twickenham on Saturday night, the 25-year-old admitted the emotions were rolling around in his brain as he lined up for the national anthems. He had been thinking about just how far he had come in a short time. It has been a whirlwind ride, that is certain — from leaving Toulon, to the charity boxing fight in Australia, a minor knee operation, a not-so-secret ski run, surviving the Canterbury earthquake, appearances for the humble Belfast club and Canterbury, and selection in the All Blacks. Williams has packed plenty into the past four months. The question for All Blacks head coach Graham Henry is what to do with him in the remaining tour matches against Scotland, Ireland and Wales ...'

MUCH like his coming-out party for the Kiwis against Australia in 2004, Sonny Bill Williams's second test for the All Blacks would be one for the ages. It was the type of performance which had the scribes once again comparing him to Jonah Lomu.

It was the type of performance that had even the cynics in the media believing the All Blacks could indeed now win the 2011 Rugby World Cup. And it was the type of performance that reminded the league fraternity, once and for all, just what they had lost because of their antiquated salary-cap system.

Indeed, the easiest storyline of the time was to evoke the name of Lomu. In *How Did I Manage That?*, Phil Kingsley Jones — Lomu's long-time manager — addressed the constant comparisons to his former charge: 'I got tired of commentators saying there was more hype around Sonny Bill Williams's debut for the All Blacks [in 2010] than there ever was before Jonah's. Well, of course there was! SBW had won an NRL title with the Bulldogs. He'd been playing professional rugby in France for two years under Tana Umaga. Then he'd been head-hunted by the All Black coaches, and every week throughout the ITM Cup we were hearing how good he was. So of course by the time of his debut against England the hype was extraordinary. Contrast that with Jonah's experience: he went from Wesley College to the All Blacks! Jonah had a Hong Kong Sevens that was impressive, but that's about it.

'When he was selected for the All Blacks, many people's first thoughts were "Who's he?" No disrespect to SBW, but we had his name rammed down our throats for 12 months before he debuted. Every man and his dog was telling us how good he would be. And I knew he would be good. And he may well become a great All Black, but will he be as good as Jonah? He will be if you listen to the critics who never gave Jonah the credit he deserved. If you listen to them, the only thing Jonah ever did was score four tries against England in the 1995 World Cup. They forget that he smashed them in the 1999 World Cup as well. They forget the try he scored in 2000 in Sydney when he danced down the sideline to score in the last minute. He was 18 stone, and he was skipping down the sideline, in limited space, like Terry Wright.

'Everyone seems to be looking for the next Jonah Lomu all of the time. But they've never found the next Jonah Lomu. Perhaps that's proof that Jonah Lomu will never be replicated. There will only ever be one Jonah Lomu.'

The build-up to the Scotland test — the second of the All Blacks' Grand Slam tour — was dominated, quite rightly, by Richie McCaw and Mils Muliaina,

The press couldn't help themselves as comparisons between Sonny Bill Williams and Jonah Lomu were made on a weekly basis during the All Blacks' tour in 2010.

who were set to join the great Sean Fitzpatrick with a record 92 test caps for the All Blacks. Such was the importance of marking the occasion with a stellar performance that the only first-choice All Black rested was the flanker Jerome Kaino.

Henry had made six changes to the starting line-up that beat the English, hooker Keven Mealamu being an enforced change after his ban for head-butting Lewis Moody during a fractious second half at Twickenham. He was replaced by Hika Elliot, Liam Messam came in for Kaino, Isaia Toeava replaced Joe Rokocoko on the right wing while the Williams experiment entered

ALL BLACKS v Scotland at Murrayfield, Edinburgh, on 13 November 2010.
All Blacks: Mils Muliaina, Isaia Toeava, Conrad Smith, *Sonny Bill Williams*, Hosea Gear, Dan Carter, Jimmy Cowan, Kieran Read, Richie McCaw (captain), Liam Messam, Sam Whitelock, Brad Thorn, Owen Franks, Hika Elliott, Tony Woodcock.
Reserves: Andrew Hore, John Afoa, Anthony Boric, Daniel Braid, Andy Ellis, Stephen Donald, Ma'a Nonu.

Sonny Bill Williams and Ma'a Nonu might be rivals for the All Blacks No. 12 jersey, but that didn't stop them sharing a joke ahead of the test against Scotland at Murrayfield in Edinburgh.

its next phase when he was named to replace Ma'a Nonu at second five-eighth. Other changes included Conrad Smith's return to centre while Jimmy Cowan regained the halfback berth from Alby Mathewson.

By the end of the 49–3 demolition of the hapless Scots, Williams had knocked McCaw and Muliaina out of the headlines with a dominant display that had the local media waxing lyrical. On the nine-minute mark Williams had burst on to a short pass and unloaded to wing Hosea Gear for a try. Two minutes later he manhandled the Scots midfield to create a turnover that led to a Dan Carter try. In the second half he set up Muliaina for a double. By the end of the game he was being awarded the Man of the Match honours.

Wynne Gray — the *New Zealand Herald*'s veteran rugby scribe — is not an easy audience. But such was Williams's dominance that Gray couldn't contain himself.

'Remember that iconic 1970 footage of Colin Meads in South Africa, sidekick Grahame Thorne in tow, mesmerising the Border defence with the ball like a peanut in his right mitt?' Gray asked his readers. 'Forty years on, Sonny Bill Williams is doing a decent impersonation of the great man. Frequently. Jonah used to clasp the pill in one duke, too, but he scarcely looked to pass or needed to.

'Every now and then there was a deft offload or skyhook lob when the big man was squeezed for room but generally he ploughed on, over or through tacklers with devastating effect. Williams is the hybrid, a fascinating mix of skill and power. He is an unpolished product, but clearly learning about rugby at such a rate of knots that, if his progress continues, he looms as a great weapon for the All Blacks.'

Gray saw Williams's single-handed carrying of the ball and offloading ability as potent weapons.

'One extraordinary flick pass against Scotland at Murrayfield held two defenders and launched Mils

Mulaina to the tryline. It is Williams's special trait, his signature move. It is the way he plays. Meads, Lomu and others like Alan Sutherland carried the pill in one hand. It was exhilarating to watch, impossible to replicate unless you had mitts the size of small pizzas. But none of them had the reverse flick, the offload which makes Williams such a threat in contact.'

Williams's potential swayed Wynne Gray:

'He has shown an ability to cope with the escalating attention, the demands of switching codes and country, life in the fishbowl world of All Black rugby, the trappings which come with an introduction to the black jersey. Containing Pinetree or Jonah at the peak of their powers would have been frightening, bottling up SBW might be just as alarming.'

More meaningful to Williams would have been the reaction of the All Blacks' backs coach Wayne Smith. 'I think he's gone well,' Smith said. 'He's different to anything we've ever seen with the way he plays. It's not the usual rugby union style and I think that's interesting to people and it's good for the team. The boys who are running in the tries off him are pretty happy about it. They're starting to understand the way he plays, they're reading his body language and trying to pick up some plums off him.'

Smith had been delighted with Williams's desire to learn. 'There are areas of his game he's got to work on but he's got a willingness to do that. He'll come into your room, he brings his book, he gets a couple of work-ons and he'll go away and work on them.'

Williams had no option but to work on them the following week when he was left out of the starting side for the test against the Irish in Dublin. Both incumbent midfield backs before the tour — Smith and Nonu — had had a test on the bench and now it

PREVIOUS PAGES: Sonny Bill Williams's best game in black came against Scotland in Edinburgh as the All Blacks cruised to a 49–3 win.
RIGHT: SBW gets an offload away during the Scotland test.

ALL BLACKS v Ireland at Lansdowne Road, Dublin, on 20 November 2010.

All Blacks: Mils Muliaina, Cory Jane, Conrad Smith, Ma'a Nonu, Hosea Gear, Dan Carter, Andy Ellis, Kieran Read, Richie McCaw (captain), Jerome Kaino, Tom Donnelly, Anthony Boric, Owen Franks, Hika Elliott, Tony Woodcock. *Reserves*: Andrew Hore, John Afoa, Sam Whitelock, Liam Messam, Alby Mathewson, Stephen Donald, **Sonny Bill Williams.**

was SBW's turn.

But there was no indication or suggestion of any missteps from Williams for his temporary demotion. It was more about experimentation than anything else. The selectors had seen him at centre and they'd seen him at second-five. Now they could judge him as an impact player.

Before the test the *Herald on Sunday*'s Dylan Cleaver — with help from Wayne Smith — tried to break down the reasons why Williams had become such a force so quickly. He told his readers that in years to come, those who saw his performance against Scotland would tell their grandchildren about the freakiest hand to ever play the sport. His analysis of Williams was broken down into six parts: instinct and vision (great game sense and awareness of where his support players are); skill (offloads, flick passes, overhead passes …); strength (ability to stand in the tackle); development (he came through a period, from age 15 to 20, in rugby league where the offload was a big part of the game); luck; and size. The last attribute includes big mitts, measuring approximately 190 mm from the tip of the thumb to the tip of his pinkie finger when outstretched. His hand is about 205 mm long and 100 mm wide. The average length of an adult male hand is 189 mm, and the average breadth is 84 mm. This all makes it easier to wrap his hand around the ball and grip it tight, so it is not as easy to

dislodge in contact, particularly when carrying the ball one-handed.

Nonu, not surprisingly, was beginning to feel the heat. He had played a big part in Williams's transition into the All Blacks but the master was in danger of being bypassed by the pupil. He was chuffed to be one of five changes to the starting line-up which carved up the Scots. Cory Jane returned from injury to replace Toeava on the right wing while Andy Ellis was named to start his first test for a year, replacing Cowan. In the pack Kaino was back for Messam and lock Tom Donnelly was back for the first time since Hong Kong in place of Sam Whitelock.

Nonu's performance in the 38–18 win in Dublin was that of a man under pressure. He was anxious. Slow on defence. Second-guessing himself on attack. He was pulled from the action with 20 minutes to go — long enough for Williams to convince Henry, Hansen and Smith that he deserved the start in the last test of the tour against Wales in Cardiff.

It was a selection that Williams coveted. But when it came his first emotion was embarrassment. 'I've always said that the more game time I get the better player I will become, but in saying that I know that I'm not the number-one 12 in the country,' Williams said. 'I know Ma'a Nonu is and what they're doing is giving me a bit more time out there to find my feet a bit more. It's not about me being selected in front of Ma'a; it's about me getting more game time to try to improve as a player. Ma'a is a good man. He's really taken me under his wing and I've learned a lot, more from him than anyone else on this tour, and he knows he's the number-one 12 in the country and he's happy for me to get some more experience. He's been there and done that.'

Henry, though, was adamant: this was a form selection. 'The team's been selected on form on the tour,' Henry emphasized. 'Ma'a Nonu has been one of the backbone members of the side for some time and he hasn't been selected in the XV for this game because Sonny Bill Williams is playing a wee bit better right now.'

Sonny Bill Williams — pictured here passing ahead of Conrad Smith — came off the bench to replace Ma'a Nonu in the win against Ireland in Dublin.

It was a massive endorsement for Williams — especially when he looked back to his first week on tour when he felt like an extra on a movie set teeming with stars. 'When I know what's going on game-plan-wise, it gives me a lot more confidence to express myself the way I want to. At the start [of the tour] I was a little bit in awe of all of them, of the silver fern.

'It is such a big brand, the All Blacks, but after a couple of weeks getting to know them, they are just boys like me, normal guys, and I started to get a little bit more comfortable. There are so many people [in the media], so many questions. But you get used to

it. It surprises me how analysed the game is. It is a worldwide game so every man and his dog have their opinions.

'Where I come from, league, it is just a two- or three-country game so it is not really over-analysed like that. With all the people talking about the All Blacks and me, there is a lot of added pressure so you have to perform every time. You don't get as much exposure in league as you do with the All Blacks. You don't get 20 people waiting outside the hotel for signatures — not for me but for the other boys, like [Dan Carter].'

For the tour-defining test against Wales, Williams

'When I know what's going on game-plan-wise, it gives me a lot more confidence to express myself the way I want to. At the start [of the tour] I was a little bit in awe of all of them, of the silver fern.'

Ma'a Nonu and Sonny Bill Williams battled for the vacant All Blacks spot alongside Conrad Smith in the All Blacks midfield on the tour. SBW won the battle by being picked for the fourth and final test against Wales, although Nonu would come on for him in the second half and be credited with turning the game in the All Blacks' favour.

ALL BLACKS v Wales at Millennium Stadium, Cardiff, on 20 November 2010.

All Blacks: Mils Muliaina, Isaia Toeava, Conrad Smith, *Sonny Bill Williams*, Hosea Gear, Dan Carter, Jimmy Cowan, Kieran Read, Richie McCaw (captain), Jerome Kaino, Sam Whitelock, Brad Thorn, Owen Franks, Keven Mealamu, Tony Woodcock.

Reserves: Andrew Hore, John Afoa, Anthony Boric, Dan Braid, Andy Ellis, Stephen Donald, Ma'a Nonu.

was one of six changes to the side that beat Ireland. Mealamu was back in the run-on side; Toeava had earned another start on the wing while Cowan regained his starting spot. In the forwards Whitelock went into the side for the injured Donnelly while Brad Thorn returned to the line-up as well.

It would be a historic line-up as the All Blacks claimed their fourth Grand Slam with a 37–25 win at Millennium Stadium. Williams had chimed in with another assist for Gear's opening try via Toeava but, in truth, it was his least effective game of the tour. But it didn't matter. Sonny Bill Williams had arrived

on rugby's world stage and he was determined to get back out there.

THE meeting was memorable for so many reasons — including being the night Sonny Bill Williams met David Tua for the first time. The venue was Monty Betham Junior's Auckland city gym. 'I couldn't believe it,' Williams said, 'I was sparring — doing some training — and in walked David Tua! What a buzz.'

Tua of course is the best boxer to come out of New Zealand. He fought for one of sports' greatest titles, the heavyweight championship of the world, in Las Vegas in 2000 when he took on Britain's Lennox Lewis. His brutal victories against John Ruiz and Michael Moorer — both at one time world champions — are the stuff of legend. His undoubted strength was recognized by the influential *Ring Magazine* which named Tua No. 48 in the all-time list of the 'world's most powerful punchers'. And more recently he stopped the nation when he took on Shane Cameron in the Fight of the Century as he proceeded to beat the bejesus out of the wannabe New Zealand No. 1. But more important than that on this night was what Tua means to fellow Samoans the world over. Like the light-heavyweight Alex Sua and the middleweights Battling La'avasa and Monty Betham before him, Tua was something of a trailblazer. His rise coincided with those of the All Blacks Michael Jones and Inga Tuigamala — three reasons for Samoans in New Zealand to embrace their culture and be outwardly proud of their roots and heritage.

'David represents so much,' Williams said. 'Everything he has done in the ring is awesome. No doubt if he wasn't so dangerous in the ring he would have challenged for the belt a few more times. A lot of guys run from him. He is the Godfather of boxing in this part of the world. So for him to come down and see me was mind-blowing ... especially because he's a fellow Samoan. As a kid I grew up watching him — being inspired by him. And then, now, there he is ... giving me advice about how to deal with adversity and

things like that. He was inspiring me all over again. Unbelievable.'

Tua said he was humbled by the meeting. 'I'm surprised he even knew who I was ...' Tua has a mantra that if he has nothing good to say, to say nothing. He didn't need to visit it on this occasion. 'I like him,' said Tua. 'I have learnt by meeting many people over many years not to judge people by the stories you hear or read about them. The only way to form a genuine opinion about someone is to meet them. When they are talking to you and you're looking them in the eye — then you know. He's something special. He's not afraid to test himself. He's not afraid of challenges. He's achieved so much already and I think that is just going to continue. It's nice of him to say I inspired him. I think he's helping to inspire a whole new generation now. And I have to say that I am very proud of the Samoan brother.'

THE most memorable game of the All Blacks' 2010 Grand Slam tour for Sonny Bill Williams was the first one. The heights he reached in his second outing in black — against Scotland — were Jonah-Lomu-esque, but for Williams nothing can beat the thrill of winning his first All Blacks jersey.

'In my first game, against England, I was probably a bit overawed — not because of the crowd but because of the team I was playing with,' he said. 'I took great satisfaction about becoming a dual international and playing with those players. I went from a year of watching them on TV to all of a sudden standing beside them, so that was pretty buzzy. Before that game, I just wanted one All Blacks jersey, but now I want to play for them as often as I can. It is such a great feeling.'

Another feeling SBW is hooked on is the thrill of being in a ring and boxing. And at the beginning of 2011 he stepped into the ring on the Gold Coast against the most respectable of any of his boxing opponents, the 'Campbelltown Bomber' Scott Lewis. The timing of the fight upset many who wondered why

David Tua was a surprise visitor to one of Sonny Bill Williams's boxing training sessions as he went through his drills in Auckland before his fight against Scott Lewis.

he was boxing at the beginning of such an important year for the All Blacks. But Williams's contract with the NZRU allows for such fights and he wasn't about to let the rugby public dictate his schedule.

'It's my first Super 15 season coming up and then obviously the World Cup, so I want to push myself, take myself out of my comfort zone instead of just having a holiday,' he said when the fight was announced. 'I feel if I do this, because it's what I've

done over the last couple of years, I'm only going to grow as a player on the field. The next six weeks are going to be about boxing, but the long-term goal is securing a spot in that World Cup squad and playing in that World Cup.'

Helping with his motivation was Lewis' record. This fight would not be a repeat of his previous two one-sided bouts. Lewis knocked out league star Carl Webb — a former Golden Glove winner — in

2010. Williams says, 'In my last bout, I was pretty disappointed afterwards and I told my manager that I'd never hop in a ring if I fought someone like that again. The other guys I fought, Gary Gurr and Ryan Hogan, weren't recognized fighters and I was embarrassed and disappointed by the Hogan fight [which lasted less than a round]. They were more exhibition bouts. It didn't show boxing the respect it deserves and made me look stupid. This one is for real. It's another challenge, it's going to keep me on my toes, but I feel that without taking risks or challenges you're not going to improve as a sportsman. I feel it's going to get the best out of me. I have just got to work hard, and it is just the same as footy; you get thrown in the deep end — in a place you don't want to be — and when you are in that deep end that is when I believe the great sportsmen separate themselves from the good sportsmen.

'About a year and a half ago, when I first put on the gloves for a proper training session, I felt really uncoordinated. I thought it was too hard. But after my first fight I had this real buzz going on and it lit a fire within me. Now, man, I love it. I try not to miss a big fight and I'm watching the sport all the time. It's in my blood.

'All of this, it's all leading towards, firstly, having a good Super Rugby season for the Crusaders and then, obviously, trying to get back in the All Blacks. This is the biggest year of my life, without a doubt. I've got a lot of goals and a lot of things I want to achieve. Obviously, I want to add boxing to my repertoire as well — I want to show that I can fight. But I also want to show that I can carry on my form from rugby last year. I'm just really looking forward to new challenges. As for doing two professional sports, it is, I guess, a

Sonny Bill Williams's third pro boxing bout was the first with any real credibility. He beat Aussie heavyweight Scott Lewis in a decision after impressing with his speed and counter-punching.

bit unprecedented. But I think that's what drives me, too. I don't just want to be your average sportsman. I want to push the boundaries and, obviously, I'm going to have my knockers but I couldn't care less. I'm doing what makes me happy and it's exciting. I'm showing that things are possible.

'That is why I believe this boxing can benefit me out on the field. What a lot of people have got to understand is, yes, I have played for the All Blacks, but I want to play for them again, and it is not set in stone that I will. I want to have a good Super 15 season, and for me to get the best out of myself, this is how I do it. Boxing has grown on me the last couple of years. I love the sport so much, and I was pretty disappointed after the last bout and frustrated that I didn't get to show what I can offer. It was disrespectful to the sport as well, so that is why I am taking on this bout. The last couple of years I have played my best rugby by boxing in the pre-season so I don't want to go away from that strategy.'

His strategy in the ring paid off against Lewis — Williams winning the six-round contest in a unanimous decision from the judges. While his punches lacked any real power, Williams did look impressive with his movement. Tony Mundine — the father of Anthony — probably took things a bit far, though, when he compared Williams to Muhammad Ali. 'I said [to Williams] in 12 months' time he could be the second Ali,' Tony said. 'I saw him 12 months ago — I really thought he moved like Ali. He needs more fights ... if he keeps on boxing seriously he will be the second Ali.'

WILLIAMS'S popularity had never been higher. It helps that he had come to terms with his missteps. 'I've had obviously the drink-driving, the thing with Candice Falzon in the toilet, getting caught pissing in the alleyway, but those things have made me who I am today, I wouldn't change that,' Williams told the *Sydney Morning Herald*.

'I think I'm evolving, I'm always in search of bettering myself, how I can improve as a sportsman and as a person. I am my own man now, I can think for myself, whereas when I was 20, 21, I always wanted to please others. I do speak my mind a lot more than when I was younger. I guess that's just my Polynesian background. That's how we are, just sit back and try to fit in, try to make everyone else happy. Now I know a lot of things in the big man's world are not what they seem, a lot of people are out for themselves and you can't always trust what someone says.

'Probably the worst thing for me, the hardest thing to overcome, has been injuries, especially when I went to France and broke my leg — that was a tough pill to take. With the other things, you can kind of blank it out. The injury is there and it's so frustrating, it gets you down. If I hadn't done those mistakes I probably wouldn't have stopped drinking. It's difficult because you've had it, you've experienced those highs and having a laugh, that's why you miss it. But it's not difficult aside from that; I know I'm better off without it. I don't make stupid mistakes; my body feels better without it.'

Being around Anthony Mundine and Khoder Nasser had also lifted his self-esteem and his confidence levels to the point where he could speak his mind. How couldn't it? Nasser is one of the most outspoken men in Australian sport. Imagine how powerful it must be for Williams to see his manager speak out in the *Sydney Morning Herald* in 2010 encouraging NRL players to strike.

'It's time for the boys to stand up and boycott the games until they get what they want,' Nasser said. 'Sonny was called "Money Bill" by some ill-informed critics — but what he is is a professional sportsman getting what he is worth on the open market. He's not being dictated to by officials who sit in their corporate boxes and eat their chocolate-fed beef. These executives are not being dictated to by a communist cap. These officials setting the rules don't have a cap on them; the coaches don't have a cap. Look at Wayne Bennett — he gets paid what he wants and then we find out he is getting even more cash from a group of businessmen who back the Broncos — the Thoroughbreds. So Mr Super Coach is earning more than his players ... a team we are told is under the cap. It's time [the players] bit the bullet and did what the boys in baseball did and went out on strike and got what they deserved. You go speak to 45-year-old ex-players with creaking joints and mounting medical bills and try to tell me that they shouldn't have got more money. Anthony Mundine realized when he was the game's biggest earner that he wasn't getting what he was worth. Why isn't the game rewarding these blokes? Why don't they conduct an audit on the NRL and find out where the money is going?'

The effect on Williams is a bulletproof self-belief. 'I am my own man, and I'm proud of that,' Williams said. 'A lot of people just say things that other people want to hear, kiss arse, but at the end of the day they're not their own man. That's what I try to stand for. I stand up for myself or if I think someone is getting treated indifferently.'

Williams's knack of pushing the boundaries has, over the years, left many people questioning his intentions. But people who know him almost always respect him. He has been a popular figure wherever he has played while he's been in the respective team's colours. And certainly he had been accepted into the All Blacks fold better than he ever dared wish for.

'They are all good blokes,' he told the *Sydney Morning Herald*, which also revealed he was now a single man after his long-term relationship with Genna Shaw ended. 'From the outside looking in, you think these guys are such big stars, but when you meet them they are just good humble blokes. You are challenging for positions, so it is pretty competitive, but at the end of the day everyone is vying for the same goal, and that is to be a winning and successful All Blacks team. Everyone wants those positions but all of the boys have a common goal, and that is to leave the jersey that you are playing in better than when you received it. [Former All Blacks flanker and skipper] Jerry Collins said that line to Jerome Kaino, and you should see how good

Jerome Kaino is playing. I am a sportsman who tries to soak up everything and take things with me as I travel along, and that is definitely one thing that has stuck with me. Every jersey that I play in from now on, I want to leave better than when I received it.'

And the chances of there being more jerseys from more teams are high. Many in New Zealand rugby hope that after the 2011 World Cup, SBW will re-sign with NZRU for a further four years. But that's unlikely as his asking price will be too high. While wearing the All Blacks jersey he has been earning only 25 per cent of what he was being paid at Toulon. And when one of your life goals is to set up your family financially for life, that's a strategy he can only afford to sign off on for 18 months.

'We've got options,' he told Fairfax. 'People look at the lifestyle of a professional athlete and see glitz and glamour, but there is a lot of hard work that goes into it, too. As a sportsman, you always want to have options. I would consider going back to league, I would consider going back to Europe and I would also consider staying in New Zealand and trying to stay in the All Blacks beyond the World Cup. But I don't know what the future holds yet and I've just got to keep working hard and concentrate on all the little goals along the way — tick the boxes, you know? I ticked a couple of boxes [in 2010] but there is still a few that need ticking this year.

'I am happy with where I am at right now and people might think it is a circus — me signing here for one year and there for one year — but at the end of the day I ain't got no one to please except me and my family, and I feel that keeping myself on my toes is the best thing for me at the moment,' he said at the beginning of 2011. 'I have been playing professional sport since I was 18 and when you are at one spot for too long it can drag on a bit, but signing short term adds pressure both ways. It keeps you on your feet and I feel it brings the best out in me.'

Rather than re-signing with the NZRU, a more likely route will be a return to rugby league via Parramatta

or South Sydney. The first option would see him link with one of his most trusted mentors, Parramatta and Kiwis coach Stephen Kearney, as well as one of his closest friends, the one-time Bulldog Reni Maitua. The latter option brings into play Nasser and Mundine's close friend, Academy Award winner Russell Crowe — the owner of South Sydney Rabbitohs. And he knows if he chooses that route rugby fans will criticize him for leaving their code and many in rugby league will want to revisit 2008 ad nauseam. And, as usual, he will be defiant. 'My career has been all about taking risks and pushing the boundaries of my ability,' he said. 'Without the risk factor I'd be bored. Where's the fun in life without the risk? It's what gets my adrenaline going. I don't like sitting back and taking easy options. No matter what I do, I'll always have my knockers. They are lining up to jump on the bandwagon to try to knock me down. But let them say what they want. I look myself in the mirror every day and I am at peace with what I see.'

Williams may opt for a 'fundraising' year in Europe first but, regardless of his arrival date at Parramatta, there is a very good chance that come the 2012 Rugby League World Cup, Williams will be vying to win his second World Cup.

For that scenario to play out, the All Blacks have to win the 2011 Rugby World Cup. And while that part of the equation isn't guaranteed, it can now be said — without howls from rugby traditionalists — that the All Blacks' chances of tasting World Cup success for the first time since 1987 are better now because of Sonny Bill Williams.

'As a sportsman, you always want to have options.
I would consider going back to league, I would consider going back to Europe and I would also consider staying in New Zealand and trying to stay in the All Blacks beyond the World Cup.'

STATISTICS

CANTERBURY-BANKSTOWN BULLDOGS

National Rugby League

2004

Round 1	v **Parramatta** 48–14 (scored a try)
Round 2	v **Cronulla** 24–20
Round 3	v **Sydney** 0–35
Round 5	v **Manly** 28–26
Round 6	v **Warriors** 24–18
Round 7	v **South Sydney** 34–8
Round 21	v **Penrith** 46–20
Round 22	v **North Queensland** 36–16 (scored a try)
Round 23	v **Brisbane** 46–18
Round 24	v **Melbourne** 12–22
Round 26	v **New Zealand** 54–10 (scored a try)
Semifinal	v **North Queensland** 22–32 (scored a try)
Semifinal	v **Melbourne** 43–18
Semifinal	v **Penrith** 30–14
Grand Final	v **Sydney** 16–13

2005

Round 1	v **St George Illawarra** 46–28
Round 2	v **North Queensland** 12–24 (scored a try)
Round 3	v **Wests Tigers** 36–37
Round 4	v **Cronulla** 12–26
Round 13	v **South Sydney** 21–21

2006

Round 6	v **South Sydney** 26–18
Round 7	v **Manly** 14–40 (scored a try)
Round 8	v **New Zealand** 30–16
Round 9	v **Sydney** 30–14 (scored a try)
Round 10	v **Parramatta** 22–18
Round 11	v **Cronulla** 32–24
Round 12	v **Brisbane** 6–26
Round 13	v **Newcastle** 38–22
Round 14	v **Canberra** 26–28
Round 15	v **North Queensland** 20–12
Round 16	v **Melbourne** 12–16 (scored a try)
Round 17	v **Wests Tigers** 32–10
Round 18	v **New Zealand** 22–18
Round 19	v **St George Illawarra** 22–16 (scored a try)
Round 20	v **Sydney** 25–0 (scored a try)
Round 22	v **North Queensland** 54–14 (scored two tries)
Round 23	v **St George Illawarra** 26–10 (scored a try)
Round 25	v **Manly** 20–21
Round 26	v **Penrith** 30–22
Semifinal	v **Canberra** 30–12
Semifinal	v **Brisbane** 20–37

2007

Round 1	v **Newcastle** 24–25
Round 4	v **South Sydney** 34–10
Round 5	v **Manly** 14–16 (scored a try)
Round 7	v **Wests Tigers** 18–34 (scored a try)
Round 8	v **Newcastle** 30–16
Round 9	v **Melbourne** 14–38
Round 10	v **Cronulla** 20–30 (scored a try)
Round 11	v **North Queensland** 16–26
Round 12	v **New Zealand** 40–20 (scored two tries)
Round 14	v **Brisbane** 12–19 (scored a try)
Round 15	v **Manly** 27–8
Round 16	v **Sydney** 38–6 (scored two tries)
Round 17	v **Cronulla** 14–12

Round 19	v **Gold Coast** 36–12
Round 20	v **St George Illawarra** 28–24
	(scored a try)
Round 21	v **Parramatta** 14–32 (scored a try)
Round 22	v **Canberra** 52–4
	(scored three tries)
Round 23	v **Brisbane** 25–24
Round 24	v **Melbourne** 6–38
Round 25	v **North Queensland** 32–38
	(scored a try)
Semifinal	v **Parramatta** 6–25

2008

Round 1	v **Parramatta** 20–28
Round 3	v **Wests Tigers** 32–12
	(scored a try)
Round 4	v **Sydney** 12–40
Round 5	v **New Zealand** 16–36
Round 6	v **St George Illawarra** 30–18
Round 7	v **Manly** 22–30 (scored a try)
Round 10	v **Gold Coast** 20–24
Round 11	v **Cronulla** 30–22 (scored a try)
Round 16	v **Sydney** 14–24
Round 17	v **South Sydney** 30–34
Round 18	v **Brisbane** 26–18 (scored a try)

BULLDOGS SUMMARY

	Played	Tries	Points
2004	15	4	16
2005	5	1	4
2006	21	8	32
2007	21	14	56
2008	11	4	16
Total	73	31	124

• Sonny Bill Williams played a total of 110 games over seven years in all grades for the Bulldogs, scoring 55 tries as well as kicking one goal (222 points).

KIWIS
Test matches

2004	v **Australia** at North Harbour 16–16
	v **Australia** at Newcastle 10–37
	v **Australia** at London 12–32
	v **Great Britain** at Huddersfield 22–12
	(scored a try)
2006	v **Australia** in Brisbane 12–50 (scored a try)
2007	v **Australia** in Brisbane 6–30
2008	v **Australia** in Sydney 12–28

RUGBY CLUB TOULONNAISE

2008–09

Top 14

Round 1	v **Clermont** 22–16	
	(scored a try)	
Round 2	v **Brive** 3–3	
Round 13	v **Montpellier** 8–33	
Round 14	v **Clermont** 5–32	
Round 15	v **Brive** 9–19	
Round 16	v **Mont-de-Marsan** 38–22	
	(scored a try)	
Round 17	v **Paris** 12–22	
Round 18	v **Bourgoin** 23–12	
Round 19	v **Bayonne** 3–3	
Round 21	v **Castres** 9–25	
Round 22	v **Montauban** 33–20	
Round 23	v **Toulouse** 14–6	
Round 25	v **Dax** 22–12	

Amlin Challenge Cup

Round 4	v **Montpellier** (France) 30–9
Round 5	v **Bristol** (England) 19–37

2009–10

Top 14

Round 13	v **Brive** 19–10
Round 14	v **Paris** 22–18
Round 15	v **Racing Metro** 28–15
Round 16	v **Albi** 41–13
Round 19	v **Montpellier** 31–19
Round 20	v **Toulouse** 6–3
Round 21	v **Biarritz** 21–20
Round 22	v **Castres** 19–6
Round 23	v **Bourgoin** 13–9
Round 25	v **Perpignan** 33–23
Round 26	v **Brive** 26–13
	(scored a try)
Semifinal	v **Clermont** 35–29
	(scored a try)

Amlin Challenge Cup

Round 3	v **Femi-CZ Rugby Rovigo** (Italy) 73–3
Round 4	v **Femi-CZ Rugby Rovigo** 30–7
Round 6	v **Castres** (France) 42–10
Quarterfinal	v **Scarlets** (Wales) 38–12
	(scored a try)
Semifinal	v **Connacht** (Ireland) 19–12
Final	v **Cardiff** (Wales) 21–28
	(scored a try)

CANTERBURY

ITM Cup

2010

Round 6	v **Bay of Plenty** 28–9
Round 7	v **Northland** 27–23
Round 8	v **Taranaki** 31–20
	(scored a try)
Round 9	v **Wellington** 37–30
	(scored a try)
Round 10	v **Otago** 35–20 (scored a try)
Round 11	v **Southland** 26–16*
Round 12	v **Counties Manukau** 39–21**
	(scored a try)

* Ranfurly Shield challenge

** Ranfurly Shield defence

ALL BLACKS

Test matches

2010	v **England** at London 26–16
	v **Scotland** at Edinburgh 49–3
	v **Ireland** at Dublin 38–18
	v **Wales** at Cardiff 37–25

BOXING 2009–11

	SBW's weight	Opponent	Venue	Result
27 May 2009	229¾ lb	**Garr Gurr** (220½ lb, Australia)	Brisbane ET, QLD	W TKO 2/4
30 June 2010	236 lb	**Ryan Hogan** (271¼ lb, Australia)	Brisbane ET, QLD	W TKO 1/4
29 January 2011	236 lb	**Scott Lewis** (223 lb, Australia)	Gold Coast, QLD	UD

W = win; TKO = technical knockout; UD = unanimous decision

ABOUT THE AUTHOR

This is John Matheson's 20th book. His previous rugby offerings have included: the bestselling trilogy with former All Black and Sevens star Eric Rush; the No. 1 bestselling biography on All Blacks great Christian Cullen; tribute books to All Blacks Tana Umaga, Andrew Mehrtens, Richie McCaw and Daniel Carter; as well as Super coach Robbie Deans; the 2007 biography with living legend Buck Shelford; and *Black Days* — a collection of interviews with the likes of Phil Kearns, Gareth Edwards, Willie John McBride, Francois Pienaar, Serge Blanco and David Campese about the experience of facing the Men in Black.

He is also the co-author of another of 2011's new offerings: Phil Kingsley Jones's biography *How Did I Manage That?*

Outside rugby, his subjects have included biographies with league stars Stacey Jones and Monty Betham, Silver Ferns netballer-cum-cancer-survivor Marg Foster, a tribute to Indy Car superstar Scott Dixon, and books on New Zealand's two successful All Whites World Cup journeys — *All Whites 82* and 2010's *All Whites Fever* — as well as an historical account of the New Zealand Warriors' first 15 years in the world's toughest league competition.

A six-time recipient at the Qantas Awards and a multiple finalist at the National Sports Journalism Awards, Matheson is now the NZ Radio Awards winning producer of Martin Devlin's top-rated sports radio show on Radio Live — 'Devlin Does Sport'. He is also a senior writer for *Truth Weekender*.

He dedicates this book to daughter Ava-Dawn — 'Heaven's gift to me.'

HarperSports

An imprint of HarperCollinsPublishers

First published in 2011

by HarperCollinsPublishers (New Zealand) Limited

PO Box 1, Shortland Street, Auckland 1140

HarperCollinsPublishers

31 View Road, Glenfield, Auckland 0627, New Zealand

25 Ryde Road, Pymble, Sydney, NSW 2073, Australia

A 53, Sector 57, Noida, UP, India

77–85 Fulham Palace Road, London W6 8JB, United Kingdom

2 Bloor Street East, 20th floor, Toronto, Ontario M4W 1A8, Canada

10 East 53rd Street, New York, NY 10022, USA

National Library of New Zealand Cataloguing-in-Publication Data

Matheson, John, 1968-

Sonny Bill Williams : the story of rugby's new superstar / John Matheson.

ISBN 978-1-86950-862-3

1. Williams, Sonny Bill, 1985-. 2. Rugby football players—New Zealand—Biography.

796.333092—dc 22

Cover and internal design by Dexter Fry

Printed by Bookbuilders, China

PHOTO CREDITS

Action Photographics:14, 15, 19, 25, 28, 33, 34, 36–37, 38, 44, 53, 67.

Fairfax: 116–117, 134–135.

Marlborough Express: 8–9.

The Press: 90–91, 92-93, 95.

TRANZ/Action Images: cover, 2, 4–5, 6–7, 10, 13, 17, 18, 20–21, 22–23, 24, 26, 27, 30, 31, 35, 41, 45, 47, 51, 55, 56–57, 59, 60, 62, 64–65, 69, 71, 72, 73, 75, 77, 78, 81, 83, 84–85, 87, 89, 98, 101, 102, 103, 105 (top), 105 (bottom), 107, 108, 109 (top), 109 (bottom left), 109 (bottom right), 110, 112–113, 114 (bottom), 118, 120, 121, 122, 123 (top), 123 (bottom), 124–125, 127, 128–129, 130, 131, 133, 138, 139, 141, back cover.

TRANZ/Zuma: 42, 48–49,114 (top).

TRANZ/Photoshot: 115.